Pressure Cooker Cookbook

100 Quick, Easy, and Healthy Pressure Cooker Recipes for Nourishing and Delicious Meals

Table of Contents

Introduction

Chapter 1 - The History and Science of the Pressure Cooker

Chapter 2 - The Health Benefits of Pressure Cooking

Chapter 3 - Choosing a Pressure Cooker

Chapter 4 - How to Use and Clean a Pressure Cooker

Chapter 5 - Converting Recipes to a Pressure Cooker

Chapter 6 - A Few More Tips

Chapter 7 – Breakfast

       Pumpkin Steel Cut Oats
       Huevos Rancheros
       Basic Hard-Boiled Eggs
       Poached Eggs in Bell Pepper Cups
       Easy Egg Pulao
       All-American Breakfast Hash
       Better-Than-Fast-Food Breakfast Burrito
       Pressure-Cooker Egg Muffins
       Choose-Your-Own-Adventure Breakfast Sandwich
       Totally-Customizable Breakfast Quinoa
       Tofu, Veggie, and Potato Hash

Chapter 8 - Chicken Entrees

       30-Minute Chicken Chickpea Masala
       Teriyaki Chicken
       Date-Night Chicken Fricassee
       Fast Chicken Bouillabaisse
       Chicken Pineapple Salad
       Spanish Chicken Fajitas

Spicy Sriracha-Honey Chicken
Lime-Salsa Mozzarella Chicken
Thai Peanut Chicken Thighs
Chicken Cacciatore

Chapter 9 - Beef Entrees

Pressure Cooker Pot Roast
Asian-Inspired Beef Ribs
Corned Beef 'n Cabbage
Mongolian Beef
Shredded Flank Steak
Beef Stroganoff
Quick Beef Tips
Pressure-Cooker Rib Eye Steak
Cheese-Stuffed Hamburgers
Classic Meatloaf
Beef Pho With Homemade Broth
Beef Osso Bucco

Chapter 10 - Seafood Entrees

Coconut Fish Curry
Pressure Cooker Shrimp Paella
Steamed Mediterranean Cod
Pressure-Cooker Mussels
Pressure-Cooker Lobster Tails
Steamed Crab Legs
Seafood Gumbo
Pressure-Cooker Creole Cod
Four White-Fish-Lemon Packets
Simple Salmon 'n Veggies
Tasty Teriyaki Salmon
Pressure-Cooker Salmon Risotto

Chapter 11 – Soups

Classic Chicken Noodle Soup
Cheesy Broccoli Soup

Clam Chowder
Pressure-Cooker Ramen
Garden Minestrone
Chicken, Chorizo, and Kale Soup
Creamy Butternut Squash and Ginger Soup
Chicken Wild Rice Soup
Tomato Basil Soup
French Onion Soup
Fast Chicken Stock
Leftover Turkey-and-Veggie Soup

Chapter 12 - Vegan Entrees

Vegan Chili
Vegan Hot Tamales
Pulled Jack-Fruit Sandwich
20-Minute Miso Risotto
Pressure-Cooker Feijoada
Pressure-Cooker Lentils
Italian Tofu Scramble
Pressure-Cooker Seitan with Red Wine Mushroom
Sauce
Black-Eyed Pea & Collard Green Chili

Chapter 13 - Side Dishes

Pressure-Cooker Cornbread
Parmesan Prosecco Risotto
Fast Potato Salad
Quinoa Almond Pilaf
Spicy Black Bean Brown Rice Salad
Roasted Cauliflower Barley Risotto
Pressure-Cooker Cheesy Potatoes
Whole White Beets with Greens
Maple-Glazed Carrots
Prosciutto-Wrapped Asparagus
Mashed Acorn Squash
Acorn Squash Stuffed with Curried Chickpeas

Chapter 14 - Snack Foods

     Pressure-Cooker "Gold Nugget" Potatoes
     Italian Popcorn
     Classic Artichoke Dip
     Sweet 'n Tender BBQ Sausage Bites
     Boiled Peanuts
     Sweet Bourbon Chicken Wings
     Applesauce in a Pressure Cooker
     Meatballs with Marinara
     Homemade Hummus
     BBQ Brisket Sliders
     Pressure-Cooker Pigs in a Blanket

Chapter 15 – Desserts

     Pressure-Cooker Peach Cobbler
     Coconut Rice Pudding
     Pressure-Cooker Pumpkin Pie
     Key Lime Pie
     Pressure-Cooked Baked Apples
     Egg-Free Chocolate Cake
     5-Minute Nut Fudge
     Baked Chocolate Custard
     Amaretti-Stuffed Peaches
     Chestnut-Hazelnut Truffles
     Pressure-Cooker Mocha Cheesecake

Epilogue

Index - Time Conversion Charts

BONUS: FREE Paleo Diet book

Introduction

In a perfect world, healthy eating would be easy. Instead of relying on packaged foods or restaurants, everyone would be able to easily prepare every meal at home using nutritious ingredients, even if they work long hours and come home exhausted. Unfortunately, cooking from scratch usually takes up a lot of time, and after a hard day, you would much rather pick up the phone and order takeout, or pop something into the microwave. Healthy diet and fitness are what I do for a living, and even I still feel tempted to lay back and let the food come to me.

Luckily for me, there is a way to make food lightning-fast and still healthy. No, it's not deep-frying, which is very unhealthy, or even steaming, which has its benefits. It is pressure-cooking! While other cooking methods destroy or leech out the nutrients inside food, the pressure cooker allows food to hold on to more vitamins because it takes significantly less time. A pressure cooker is able to safely cook food so fast because it raises the boiling point of water by applying pressure. Instead of plateauing out at about 212-degrees Fahrenheit, water is able to reach temperatures of 257-degrees, thereby quickly cooking meats, veggies, and more.

This often-forgotten piece of kitchen equipment can be used to make just about every kind of meal (including dessert), and it has proven itself to be the best cooking method in terms of vitamin retention. You can get the most out of vegetables like broccoli and peas, and barely lift a finger. It is also the fastest method of cooking, and cuts of meat that would normally take hours cook up three times as quickly. Unlike slow cookers, which offer a similar hands-off convenience, you don't have to think of and prepare meals hours ahead. Making a meal like spicy chicken curry with rice can take a total of 30 minutes with a pressure cooker. You can maintain a hectic schedule *and* still eat healthy, filling meals.

Whether you are familiar with pressure cookers or not, this book provides you with 100 easy, convenient pressure-cooker dishes for every meal of the day. The earlier chapters help break down some of the science of pressure cooking, as well as how to choose the right pressure cooker and how to use one. By the time you've finished this book, you will be more than ready to cook your first pressure cooker meal, whether it's a hearty vegetarian chili, sweet breakfast quinoa, or game day-ready turkey meatballs.

Chapter 1 - The History and Science of the Pressure Cooker

Believe it or not, the first pressure cooker was not made by a chef. Denis Papin was actually a mathematician and physicist in the late 17th-century, and it was his skills as a scientist that allowed him to make a cast-iron pot that raised the boiling point of water. This pot sped up cooking meat and was even able to soften bones into a delicious, meaty jelly. Papin called it a "bone digester" or "steam digester." After creating a safety valve that prevented explosions, Papin prepared a feast for the Royal Society and King Charles II himself. The pressure cooker was met with rave reviews.

The history of the pressure cooker takes a bit of a side road at this point. It was 1795, and the French army needed preserved food supplies. A French confectioner, lured by the promise of a 12,000 franc-reward, came up with a preservation method that consisted of sealing jars with food and boiling them. Nicolas Appert won the prize and used the cash to open the world's first cannery.

Pressure canning continued to be extremely popular, and by 1917, Americans were realizing that they could make ready-to-eat meals in their pressure canners, too! At the 1939 World's Fair in New York, Presto introduced their brand's pressure cooker with a super convenient interlocking cover, free of clamps. By 1941, the pressure cooker business was booming and 11 companies were getting in on the game. WWII put a temporary halt on production, leaving home chefs impatient for a way to make fast and easy meals. When the war ended, it was difficult to find a good pressure cooker, and it seemed like this innovative tool was going by the wayside.

Lucky for me and other people who like being able to cook quick, healthy meals, the best pressure cooker companies kept trucking along, and in the 1970's, new safety features, modern styling, and pressure cooker cookbooks helped boost the popularity of the pressure cooker once again. The pressure has come a long way from the explosion-prone "bone digester," and has become one of the best ways to prepare your own healthy meals from scratch without the wait.

So, how does a pressure cooker actually work? Well, to start, you have to know a little bit about how water and heat work. The boiling point of water is 212-degrees Fahrenheit, and that's how hot the steam gets. Normally, the steam doesn't get any hotter, it can't go any higher than "boiling." The purpose of a pressure cooker, however, is to raise that temperature. By tightly locking the steam inside the pot, the pressure builds, and the overall temperature in the pot rises. An important abbreviation to know is "psi," which is the US Customary unit for pressure at sea level. It stands for pounds per inch. The normal boiling point has 14.696 psi, so a higher psi means a higher temperature, e.g. 15 psi results in a temperature of 257-degrees Fahrenheit. The next chapter will dig into the benefits of pressure cooking, and why adding a pressure cooker to your kitchen is good for your health.

Chapter 2 - The Health Benefits of Pressure Cooking

Now comes time for the million-dollar question: Is pressure cooking healthy? Lots of people are wary of the very high temperatures involved in pressure cooking, and worry that all the food nutrients are being obliterated. The reality is that pressure cooking is actually the healthiest method of cooking food!

In a 1995 study, researchers discovered that pressure cooking was the best way to preserve the beta-carotene and ascorbic acid in amaranth and spinach. Beta-carotene, which becomes vitamin A in the body, promotes healthy skin, good eyesight, and it also lowers your chances of getting heart disease. Ascorbic acid, more commonly known as the all-powerful Vitamin C, is fantastic for just about every problem, including a weak immune system, heart issues, diabetes, and even cancer. In 2007, another study confirmed the power of the pressure cooker: when cooked this way, broccoli keeps a whopping 90% of its Vitamin C, compared to the 78% when steamed and 66% when boiled.

How does this work, you ask? There are three reasons:

- Short cooking time preserves nutrients
- Less water means more nutrients
- Food is more easily digested than with other cooking methods

When food is cooked for a shorter period of time, more of the nutrients stay put. It doesn't matter if the temperature is significantly higher than normal; if the nutrients are delicate enough to be destroyed by heat, other cooking methods would destroy them, too.

What about this water thing? When you cook food in water, the nutrients leak out, and then you're just left with vegetables that are basically just shells of what they could be. Pressure cookers use less water than other cooking methods, including traditional steaming, so those food nutrients stay where they belong.

The third reason has to do with how the human body digests nutrients. Certain foods, like grains and legumes, are harder for the body to digest. Pressure cooking makes it easier by reducing certain acids that make these foods tough. Phytic acid is one of these bad guys. It ties up nutrients in the digestive system, so you don't enjoy any of the benefits. By pressure cooking phytic-acid high foods like peas after soaking them overnight, you can reduce that acid up to 54%! If that wasn't good enough, pressure cooking also makes the protein in food more easily digested. Those same peas have a protein digestibility of 84%, as opposed to the 81% they get when you soak them and boil them normally.

Chapter 3 - Choosing a Pressure Cooker

I know what you're thinking. "Pressure cookers are great! But how do I know which one to choose?" The first step is to consider the advantages and disadvantages of a stove top or electric pressure cooker. This is what a standard stove top pressure cooker looks like next to an electric one:

Stove top pressure cookers have several advantages over electric ones. For one thing, they're cheaper. They also generally have a higher psi, and last longer than electric pressure cookers, because there are no electrical components that wear out over time. On the other hand, you have to babysit stove top pressure cookers and monitor the pressure yourself. This isn't hard - you just use the quick-release on the pressure regulator - but if you want to leave the pressure cooker to do other chores, your meal might not turn out the way you want it to.

Basically, if you want an affordable, powerful pressure cooker that cooks food really fast, and you don't mind hovering around the stove, a stove top pressure cooker is probably the best choice.

Electric pressure cookers are great if you like to be hands-off in the kitchen. Just throw in your ingredients, set the pressure and timer, and you're ready to go. It's a little like a crockpot that way. There's also more safety features, and many have pre-set functions for food like beans or pot roast. Electric pressure cookers don't work for everybody, though. They tend to cost more, and they max out at about 11 psi, so cooking takes longer than with a stove top pressure cooker.

If you're a very busy person who is willing to spend a little more cash for a very safe pressure cooker that lets you set the pressure and go do other things, an electric pressure cooker is what you're looking for.

The most significant difference between stove top pressure cookers and electric pressure cookers is cooking time. Converting recipes can be tricky, so I've included a handy chart in the index that can help you out with common foods.

Once you've chosen between going stove top or electric, there are several other features you'll want to check out:

- Capacity
- Construction material
- Ease of use

What size pressure cooker should you get? It depends on the size of your family. If there's just two of you, or you cook for one, a 4-quart pressure cooker would be a good size, but if you plan on entertaining at all, you'll want a 6-quart. 6-quart pressure cookers are the most popular. The next size up is the 8-quart, which is ideal for big families. You can even buy pressure cookers up to 23-quarts, which are usually used if you're a professional who cans meats and broth.

Construction matters. The cheapest pressure cookers are usually made of aluminum, but if you want your pressure cooker to last, you'll want to go with stainless steel. Stainless steel is a lot more durable and easy to clean. The problem with stainless steel is that when it gets heated up, it becomes inconsistent, with hot and cold spots. Manufacturers have found an easy fix. Check the bottom of the pot - you'll want a pressure cooker built with a layer of aluminum, which ensures even heating.

The last thing to look for is ease of use. Can you lift the pressure cooker comfortably? Is setting the pressure (if it's an electric cooker) simple? The only way to *really* know if a pressure cooker is easy to use is once you've actually bought it and used it, but there are certain features you can check out right away. Are the handles designed well so your hands fit and aren't pinched? Is the pressure indicator easy to see or do you have to peer into a hole? Cleaning and maintaining a pressure cooker is another big part of ease of use. It may be tempting to go with non-stick, because it wipes clean so easily, but non-stick surfaces are known to chip off and wear down quickly.

Chapter 4 - How to Use and Clean a Pressure Cooker

So, you've gone out and gotten yourself a pressure cooker, so now it's time to learn how to use one. Here is a relatively simple diagram explaining the parts of a stove top, standard pressure cooker:

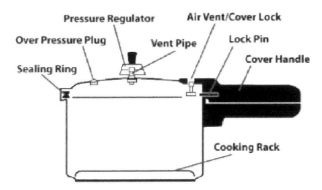

The pressure regulator is responsible for keeping all that pressure contained. It will let you know when the ideal pressure is reached. It separates from the pressure cooker, so be sure you keep it with the pressure cooker in storage, or in another place you won't forget. The vent pipe is there so you can release any excess pressure. If something goes wrong with the vent pipe, the over pressure plug is there to take over, so you never have to worry about explosions. The air vent/cover lock and lock pin are partners: when the pressure inside the cooker builds up, the air vent/cover lock allows the lock pin to pop up, locking the cover shut. The sealing ring is also there to ensure that the pressure cooker cover and pot are tightly closed. Lastly, many pressure cookers have a cooking rack, which lets you separate foods that you don't want to blend together.

Now it's time to make your first pressure cooker meal. You have your recipe and ingredients. Time is a little weird with pressure cooker cookbooks and cooking time. If it says to cook for "0 minutes," that means you cook the meal until 15 psi is reached, and then you cool. "Cool immediately" and the "cold water method" means you run the pot under cold water, so the pressure drops right away, while "cool naturally" or other similar phrasings, mean you just remove the pot from the stove top and let the pressure go down on its own. Another term for "quick release" is "normal release," which may be a bit confusing. Other terms for "quick release" are "automatic," "manual," and "regular."

Once you feel comfortable with the cooking time and cooling method, start your meal by pouring the correct amount of liquid into the pressure cooker and then add the rest of the ingredients. Before you start the cooker, just make sure the vent pipe is free of clogs. Put the cover on securely and start heating on a stove top, on high. This is where the pressure regulator is absolutely necessary - it will let you know when the 15 psi is reached. If it starts to get higher, just turn down the heat on your stove top.

Congratulations on preparing your first pressure cooker meal! I hope it was as delicious as it was nutritious. Clean-up is next, and that's never fun, but it can be pretty easy. One common problem with pressure cookers is that bits of food get stuck inside. Instead of scraping away or soaking for hours, you can actually "cook off" the bits. Pour enough water into the pot so all the food bits are covered. Add ¼ cup of white vinegar and heat until the water is boiling. You don't have to cover the pressure cooker. Once the water is boiling, turn off the heat and add a teaspoon or so of baking soda. Wait until this mixture is cool to the touch, and then rub around the pot. The food bits should be softened and come off easily. Pour out the cleaning mixture, rinse well, and that's it!

Another problem many pressure-cooker owners face is dealing with the smelly ghosts of meals past. Even after you've cleaned your pressure cooker, sometimes meals you've made before have a way of sneaking into new food. Avoiding this is very easy - just don't store your pressure cooker with the lid on. Leave a little space, so the pot can air out.

Chapter 5 - Converting Recipes to a Pressure Cooker

Since lots of people don't have a pressure cooker, most of their favorite recipes are usually made in the oven, on a burner, or in a slow cooker. When you start using a pressure cooker, you'll want to know how to convert recipes. There are lots of websites that include "Recipe Calculators," where you list the ingredients in the original recipe and the website lets you know how to cook everything in the pressure cooker. When you buy a pressure cooker, the owner's manual also usually includes a section on how to translate slow cooker recipes. However, for your convenience, let's take a look at the basics when it comes to converting any recipe to a pressure cooker. Here are the four most important questions you should be asking:

- How much cooking time does the original recipe call for?
- How much liquid does the final product include?
- Which veggies are "aromatic" and should therefore be cooked first?
- Will all the food fit into the pressure cooker or do I need to do two batches?

Pressure cooking is much faster than other methods. Find out the cook time for the original recipe (not the total prep time) and reduce it by ⅔. That's how long you will cook the meal in the pressure cooker.

The next step is to look at the liquid. Determine how much liquid the recipe ends up with, not how much you actually add. This is because other cooking methods result in a lot of evaporated liquid, while pressure cooking keeps most of the liquid. Write down how much liquid you want in the end product, plus an additional ½ cup. This will be used before you add the other ingredients, because the pressure cooker needs it to generate pressure.

Look at the vegetables in the recipe and determine which are "aromatic." These include celery, onions, garlic, carrots, and peppers. In a pressure cooker, you should always sauté these veggies first with a coat of oil on the bottom, so you can create a lovely flavor base for the rest of your ingredients.

If necessary, divide up the original recipe in half. Pressure cookers may hold less food than the usual container you use. For safety, a pressure cooker should only be filled ⅔ of the way at a time. If your meal is bigger than this, you'll need to make it in two batches.

Once you have answered these four questions, follow the recipe as it is written in terms of what order to put in ingredients and how much spice to use. If you are still uncertain about a recipe, try to find a similar one that is specifically for a pressure cooker. You can compare what you came up with to the other recipe's instructions and make any adjustments if necessary.

Chapter 6 - A Few More Tips

Before you get started, here are a few more tips that will make using a pressure cooker easier:

Safety

- Pressure cookers get very hot, so you need to exercise caution. Be especially careful when making foods that "froth," since that froth can block the steam valve. Some of these foods include oatmeal, pasta, and peas.
- You should also avoid using too much oil or attempting to "fry" foods. Use just enough oil to coat the bottom of the pressure cooker.
- Don't overfill - when you read recipes, you'll notice most only require about 1-1 ½ cup of cooking liquids. This is because using too much liquid results in less flavorful foods. Overfilling can also prevent the pressure from releasing properly.
- When you're handling the pressure cooker, always use pot holders.
- When you're using the quick-release, turn your face away from the steam, because it will be very hot.

Pantry

What items should you always have on hand if you have a pressure cooker? Though you can cook just about anything in a pressure cooker, certain foods cook better and are easier. As a general rule, any recipe that cooks really fast (eggs, noodles) and recipes that take a really long time (beef ribs) are best in the pressure cooker.

Dairy ingredients like milk, cheese, and so on should be added *after* everything else has been prepared in the pressure cooker, because these foam a lot and burn easily.

Here's a sample shopping list of foods that turn out really well in a pressure cooker:

- Tough cuts of meat, e.g. chuck steaks, shanks, brisket
- Thick cuts of meat
- Meat bones (for stock)

- Onions
- Beans
- Rice
- Quinoa
- Potatoes
- Carrots
- Chicken stock
- White wine
- Squash
- Steel-cut oats
- Eggs
- Garlic
- Chicken thighs
- Variety of spices

We've covered the history and basic science of the pressure cooker, as well as all the health benefits of pressure cooking, how to choose the right pressure cooker, and what foods cook best. Now it's time for the fun part! The rest of this book is packed with healthy and delicious pressure cooker recipes, from breakfast to snacks to desserts.

Chapter 7 - Breakfast

Pumpkin Steel Cut Oats
Serves: 6
Time: 25-30 minutes

This take on steel-cut oats is perfect for the fall and winter seasons, when you just want a bowl of something hot and sweet. It tastes just like pumpkin pie! It's also gluten-free, so if that's a concern in your family, you don't have to worry about making another breakfast.

Ingredients:
3 cups water
1 cup pumpkin puree
1 cup steel-cut oats
1 tablespoon butter
¼ cup maple syrup
2 teaspoons cinnamon
1 teaspoon pumpkin pie spice
A dash of salt

Directions:
1. Melt butter in the pressure cooker. If you're using an electric pressure cooker, select the "sauté" option.
2. Once the butter is melted, add the oats. Stir constantly for about three minutes or until toasted.
3. Add the pumpkin puree, seasonings, maple syrup, and water. Cook for ten minutes on the high pressure. If you're using a stove top pressure cooker, the cook time will likely be less, because the pressure is higher on stove top cookers. For a guide, check out the pressure cooker conversion chart at the end of this book.
4. When the cooking time is complete, remove from heat (or turn off heat) and let the pot cool naturally for about 10 minutes. If there's still leftover pressure, use the quick-release.
5. When all the pressure is gone, stir the oats.
6. Rest the oats, uncovered, for about ten minutes while the oats thicken up.
7. Serve with more maple syrup, milk, or your favorite granola!

Nutrition Info (Per Serving):

Calories - 98
Protein - 2
Fat - 3
Carbs - 18
Fiber - 3

Huevos Rancheros
Serves: 1-2
Time: 30 minutes (electric pressure cooker)

This Mexican dish combines eggs, tortillas, and salsa to create a spicy, protein-packed breakfast. You can also add ingredients like avocado or beans. Cooking the eggs in a pressure cooker, as opposed to the traditional frying, saves a lot of calories. In terms of equipment, you need a vegetable steamer attachment for the pressure cooker.

Ingredients:
3 eggs
½-¾ cup salsa
Tortillas (or tortilla chips)
Salt and pepper

Directions:
1. In a ramekin or other small dish, mix half a cup of salsa.
2. In a separate container, crack the eggs.
3. Add eggs on top of salsa.
4. Wrap the ramekin in foil, so the whole thing is tightly-packed. You don't want hot water to get into the ramekin.
5. Pour one cup of cold water into the vegetable steamer (after taking out the center prong) and put the steamer in the pressure cooker.
6. Put the wrapped ramekin with eggs and salsa on top of the steamer, and then lock the pressure cooker lid.
7. Cook at low pressure (around 6 psi) for 20 minutes, using the quick-pressure release if the pressure starts to build too much.
8. Arrange the warm tortilla or chips on a plate and when ready, spoon out the eggs and salsa on top. The ramekin will be hot, so don't touch with your bare hands.
9. Add beans, avocado, or more salsa if you want.

Nutrition Info (Per Serving):

Calories - 243
Protein - 16
Fat - 11
Carbs - 22
Fiber - 4

Basic Hard-Boiled Eggs
Serves: 8 (one egg per person)
Time: 46 minutes

A hard-boiled egg is one of the best breakfasts you can have. It fills you up more than cereal or bread, and doesn't have the high number of calories that those foods have. In terms of nutrition, eggs are packed with protein, which is a great way to jump start your day! By boiling a whole bunch at once in a slow cooker, you have breakfasts for a whole week if it's just you.

Ingredients:
8 eggs
2 cups of water
4 cups of cold water
4 cups ice cubes

Directions:
1. Start by filling the pressure cooker with the minimum amount of water recommended by the pressure cooker's manual.
2. Put all 8 eggs in the steamer basket. Seal the pressure cooker.
3. Heat until the lowest pressure is reached.
4. Cook for 6 minutes. Do not let the pressure get too high, or the eggs will crack.
5. After 6 minutes, remove from heat and let the pressure drop naturally for about 5 minutes.
6. In a large bowl, mix the ice and cold water.
7. Carefully move the eggs to the ice water.
8. Cool for 30 minutes.
9. Peel and eat, or store.

Nutrition Info (Per Serving):
Calories - 211
Protein - 17
Fat - 14

Carbs - 2
Fiber - 0

Poached Eggs in Bell Pepper Cups
Serves: 2
Time: 15 minutes

This rich and cheesy egg dish is great for a homemade brunch with a friend or as a romantic breakfast-for-dinner date. If you're feeling particularly ambitious, you can even make your own Hollandaise sauce very quickly. You will need a steamer basket for your pressure cooker.

Ingredients:
2 eggs
2 bell peppers
2 pieces of toasted whole-grain bread
2 slices of smoked Gouda
1 small bunch of greens

Directions:
1. Pour one cup of water into the pressure cooker.
2. Prepare the bell pepper by cutting the ends so they look like cups about 1 ½-inches high.
3. Crack the eggs, one in each cup.
4. Wrap tightly in foil and place in the steamer basket in the pressure cooker.
5. Seal the lid.
6. You want low pressure for this recipe, so once the lowest pressure is reached, cook for 3-4 minutes.
7. When ready, release the pressure inside the cooker manually.
8. On a plate, lay down the toast, cheese, and greens before putting the egg-and-pepper cups on top of everything. Add Hollandaise if desired.

To make the Hollandaise:
This is a "mock" Hollandaise, but it tastes just as good. Whisk together ⅔ cup mayo, 3 tablespoons orange juice, 1 tablespoon white wine vinegar, 1½ teaspoons Dijon mustard, 1 teaspoon lemon juice, 1 teaspoon turmeric, and a dash of salt.

Nutrition Info (Per Serving/No Hollandaise):

Calories - 326
Protein - 21
Fat - 13
Carbs - 35
Fiber - 0

Easy Egg Pulao
Serves: 3
Time: 10-30 minutes

Egg Pulao is a south Indian dish that is perfect for a filling breakfast, lunch, or dinner, but it's included here as a breakfast because it uses boiled eggs. When you boil the eggs and soak the rice beforehand, the whole recipe takes less than ten minutes. This is for a stove top pressure cooker.

Ingredients:
3-4 hard-boiled eggs
2 ½ cups of water
1-2 green chilies
1 medium-sized onion, sliced thin
1 ½ cups of Basmati rice
1 cup mixed veggies (like carrots, potatoes, peas)
2-3 tablespoons oil
Pinch of garam masala powder
1 ½ teaspoons ginger garlic paste
Salt to taste

Directions:
1. Peel the eggs and pierce with a fork.
2. Mince the chilies.
3. Heat oil in a pressure cooker before adding spices.
4. Add the onions and fry. When they are just beginning to caramelize, add the ginger garlic paste.
5. Add veggies and cook for two minutes.
6. Add garam masala powder and chili and fry for another two minutes.
7. Pour in water and salt to taste until it boils.
8. If you want the eggs to have more flavor, you can fry them in a little bit of oil in a separate pan.
9. Add the rice to the pressure cooker.
10. Cover the pressure cooker and turn the stove top to medium. When the cooker reaches pressure, remove from heat.

11. Once the pressure has naturally gone down, plate and add eggs on top.

Nutrition Info (Per Serving):
Calories - 218
Protein - 17
Fat - 10
Carbs - 20
Fiber - 1

All-American Breakfast Hash
Serves: 4
Time: About 30 minutes

This is not a low-calorie meal, but if you want a Saturday-morning hearty, lumberjack-style breakfast or brunch that only uses 4 ingredients, pressure cooking is an easy and delicious way to prepare it.

Ingredients:
6 beaten eggs
6 small, shredded potatoes
1 cup cooked breakfast ham, chopped
1 cup shredded Cheddar cheese

Directions:
1. Coat the bottom of your pressure cooker with oil and warm.
2. Place shredded potatoes in cooker and let them brown.
3. Beat the eggs in a separate, pressure-cooker safe container. Add ham. Wrap tightly in foil.
4. Mix the browned potatoes in the pressure cooker with 1 cup of water. Be careful not to splatter yourself.
5. Place the wrapped egg and ham in the pressure cooker steamer.
6. Cook until the lowest pressure is reached.
7. Carefully check eggs. If they're not at your preferred doneness, cook a little longer.
8. Plate potatoes and add eggs on top. Sprinkle with cheese.

Nutrition Info (Per Serving):
Calories - 356
Protein - 22

Fat - 18
Carbs - 25
Fiber - 3

Better-Than-Fast-Food Breakfast Burrito
Serves: 4
Time: <10 minutes

This breakfast burrito is packed with high-protein beans, eggs, and vitamins from the tomato and avocado. Like the recipe above, it's not for those seeking few calories, but it's probably filling enough to serve as breakfast and lunch.

Ingredients:
8 diced hard-boiled eggs
4 whole-grain tortillas
1 cup black beans
½ cup diced tomato
¼ cup chopped cilantro
¼ cup diced red onion
¼ cup water
2 tablespoons olive oil
1 peeled and sliced avocado
1 teaspoon salt
Optional: Shredded cheese and sour cream

Directions:
1. Heat the olive oil in the pressure cooker.
2. Add eggs and stir until coated in oil.
3. After a few minutes, add tomato, cilantro, onion, water, and salt.
4. Lock the lid and maintain high pressure for 6 minutes.
5. Remove from heat and quick-release.
6. Warm the tortillas in the microwave.
7. Prepare burrito by arranging ¼ of the pressure-cooker mixture, ¼ of the beans, and ¼ of the avocado in a line along the middle of the tortilla.
8. Roll the burrito.
9. Top with optional ingredients.

Nutrition Info (Per Serving):
Calories - 394
Protein - 21

Fat - 25
Carbs - 19
Fiber - 11

Pressure-Cooker Egg Muffins
Serves: 4 (one muffin each)
Time: 10 minutes

These egg muffins flecked with bacon, green onion, and cheese are perfect if you're on the go and need something portable. If you don't have silicone muffin cups, you can use ramekin dishes for more of an individual quiche feel.

Ingredients:
4 eggs
1 diced green onion
4 strips crumbled bacon
4 tablespoons shredded cheddar cheese
¼ teaspoon lemon pepper seasoning
1 ½ cups water

Directions:
1. Add 1 ½ cups of water to the pressure cooker.
2. Beat eggs in a bowl with seasoning.
3. Even divide the cheese, crumbled bacon, and green onion between four silicon muffin cups (or ramekins).
4. Add the beaten egg and stir to blend ingredients.
5. Put the cups into the steamer basket attachment inside the pressure cooker.
6. Secure lid and cook on high pressure for 8 minutes.
7. When time is up, wait two minutes, and then use the quick-release.
8. Serve egg muffins. They can also be stored in the refrigerator for a week or so.

Nutrition Info (Per Serving):
Calories - 185
Protein - 16
Fat - 16
Carbs - 0
Fiber - 11

Choose-Your-Own-Adventure Breakfast Sandwich

Serves: 1
Time: 10 minutes

This sandwich is totally customizable, so you can make it as healthy or decadent as you want. By cooking the main sandwich ingredients in the pressure cooker, you create a hot, energy-packed breakfast in minutes. Pair with your favorite whole-grain bread to complete the meal.

Ingredients:
1 cup water
1 thin slice prosciutto (or other breakfast meat like ham or roast beef)
1 egg
Splash of olive oil (or coconut oil or butter)
1 tablespoon shredded cheese (or your choice)
2 slices bread

Directions:
1. Add water to pressure cooker.
2. Pour in oil to coat the bottom of your ramekin, which is where the ingredients will cook.
3. Pile (in this order) meat, egg, and cheese in the ramekin. You can use a whole egg or scrambled.
4. Cover the ramekin tightly with foil and place in steamer attachment in pressure cooker.
5. Cook on the lowest pressure for 6 minutes.
6. Remove from heat and let it naturally decrease.
7. Toast your bread.
8. Make your sandwich!

Nutrition Info (Per Serving):
Calories - 277
Protein - 17
Fat - 12
Carbs - 26
Fiber - 0

Totally-Customizable Breakfast Quinoa
Serves: 4
Time: 7 minutes

You've probably had quinoa as a side dish at dinnertime, but did you know you can also eat it for breakfast? Quinoa is a healthy alternative to oats and cooks really fast in a pressure cooker. You can customize this recipe to your liking and add anything from raspberries to coconut flakes to chocolate chips, depending on your mood.

Ingredients:
1 ½ cups quinoa
2 cups of water
1 tablespoon oil
Honey to taste
Optional add-ins: Cinnamon, coconut flakes, fresh fruit, fruit preserves, chocolate chips

Directions:
1. Add the water, quinoa, and oil into the pressure cooker.
2. Secure lid tightly.
3. Bring to high pressure and cook for 7 minutes.
4. When the timer goes off, remove from heat and use the quick-release.
5. Drain quinoa.
6. Sweeten with honey or your favorite sweetener.
7. Mix in optional add-ins and enjoy!

Nutrition Info (Per Serving/Without Toppings):
Calories - 270
Protein - 8
Fat - 7
Carbs - 44
Fiber - 6

Tofu, Veggie, and Potato Hash
Serves: 4
Time: 3 minutes

If speed is a priority for you, this vegetarian breakfast hash is right up your alley. Once the veggies are peeled and chopped, cooking only takes about 2 minutes followed by a minute of pressure release. You can make the dish your own by adding your favorite spice blend to give it a Mexican, Indian, or Italian flair.

Ingredients:

½ pound firm, cubed tofu
1 diced onion
2-3 fingerling potatoes, cut into 1-inch chunks
1 piece minced ginger root
1 peeled, cut carrot
1 tablespoon soy sauce
2-3 tablespoons of chicken broth
1 ½ cups of veggies
Spices to taste

Directions:

1. Dry sauté the onion for about a minute. As soon as the onion starts to stick to the bottom of the pressure cooker, add a tablespoon of water.
2. Throw in the potatoes, carrot, soy sauce, ginger, and tofu. Sauté for 1 minute.
3. Add the spices and leftover water.
4. Secure the pressure cooker lid and bring to the highest pressure. Maintain for 2 minutes.
5. Once the timer goes off, quick-release. If you have any faster-cooking vegetables like spinach, add now.
6. Secure the lid again and maintain high pressure for 1 minute.
7. Quick release the pressure a last time.
8. Serve!

Nutrition Info (Per Serving):
Calories - 138
Protein - 12
Fat - 3
Carbs - 21
Fiber – 1

Chapter 8 - Chicken Entrees

30-Minute Chicken Chickpea Masala
Serves: 4
Time: 40 minutes

This traditional Indian dish is blooming with fragrant spices, a rich sauce, and protein-packed chickpeas and lean chicken. Thanks to the pressure cooker, you can get deep flavors that would ordinarily require a long simmering time, in just a half-hour. Allow about 10 minutes for prepping.

Ingredients:
3 pounds chicken thighs and drumsticks
1 pound fresh spinach
 2 15-ounce cans of chickpeas
1 cup diced onions
4 minced garlic cloves
1 15-ounce can of tomatoes
½ cup chicken stock
½ cup heavy cream
½ cup chopped cilantro
¼ cup fresh lemon juice
2 tablespoons butter
1 tablespoon grated ginger
1 tablespoon ground cumin
1 ½ teaspoons ground coriander
1 ½ teaspoons paprika
1 teaspoon ground turmeric
¼ teaspoon cayenne
Dash of salt and black pepper

Directions:
1. Heat butter over medium-high heat (if using a stove top pressure cooker) or "sear" for an electric pressure cooker.
2. When the butter stops foaming, add the garlic, ginger, and onions.
3. After about 5 minutes or until the ingredients are pale brown, add the spices.
4. When the spices have "bloomed," or after 30 seconds, add the spinach and can of tomatoes.
5. Cover and cook until the spinach is wilted.

6. Add the chicken stock, half of the cilantro, and chicken. Stir.
7. Secure the pressure cooker tightly.
8. Cook for 15 minutes on high pressure.
9. Once cooled, release the pressure.
10. Add the cream, chickpeas (drained), lemon juice, and let it simmer until thickened.
11. Season with salt and the rest of the lemon juice.
12. Serve right after, sprinkled with the rest of the cilantro.

Nutrition Info (Per Serving):
Calories - 845
Protein - 66
Fat - 59
Carbs - 11
Fiber – 4

Ginger Chicken
Serves: 4
Time: 25 minutes

This six-ingredient, six-step chicken dish is an easy homemade alternative to the MSG-packed, high-sodium you would find at most Chinese takeout places. It also takes about just as long as waiting for the takeout, from prep to serving!

Ingredient:
32-ounces of chicken (cut up)
1 piece of fresh ginger, grated
1 onion, diced
¼ cup soy sauce
¼ cup dry sherry
¼ cup water

Directions:
1. Coat the bottom of the pressure cooker with oil and heat.
2. Brown chicken.
3. Add onion and ginger and stir.
4. Add the water, soy sauce, and sherry.
5. Secure the pressure cooker lid and maintain 15 psi for 6 minutes, or 10 psi for 8 minutes.
6. Serve with white rice or quinoa.

Nutrition Info (Per Serving):

Calories - 315
Protein - 22
Fat - 6
Carbs - 46
Fiber - 0

Teriyaki Chicken

Serves: 8
Time: 40 minutes

Another Asian-inspired chicken dish! This one has a few more ingredients, like sweet crushed pineapple, but it's still extremely easy to make. You also make your own teriyaki sauce. To save on poultry, you can use only chicken thighs if you'd like, or a mix of thighs and breasts.

Ingredients:
3 pounds chicken
1 20-oz can of crushed pineapple
1 cup chicken stock
¾ cup of brown sugar
¾ cup soy sauce
¼ cup apple cider vinegar
2 tablespoons cold water
2 tablespoons cornstarch
2 tablespoons ground ginger
2 tablespoons garlic powder
1 teaspoon black pepper

Directions:
1. Mix sugar, soy sauce, ginger, garlic, pepper, and crushed pineapple with the juice, stock, and vinegar in a bowl until the sugar is dissolved.
2. Arrange chicken in the pressure cooker and add sauce. Stir to coat.
3. Cook on high pressure and maintain for 20 minutes.
4. In a separate bowl, mix cornstarch and cold water.
5. Quick-release the pressure.
6. Remove the chicken with tongs, leaving the sauce in the pressure cooker.
7. Whisk the cornstarch-water mixture into the sauce. This will thicken it.
8. Bring to a boil and cook for about 3 minutes. Stir frequently.

9. Plate chicken and pour over sauce.
10. You can serve the chicken on its own, with rice, or mixed veggies.

Nutrition Info (Per Serving):
Calories - 365
Protein - 45
Fat - 11
Carbs - 18
Fiber - 0

Date-Night Chicken Fricassee
Serves: 2
Time: About 20 minutes

Nothing says "I love you" quite like a home-cooked meal. Even if you aren't the best chef in the world, this rustic, pressure-cooker chicken fricassee (which is the process of cooking meat in a white sauce) has the feel and taste of an elegant restaurant dish. Portions are generous, so you can expect leftovers.

Ingredients:
4 skinned chicken leg quarters
1 pound quartered cremini mushrooms
1 pound baby carrots (peeled, with 1-inch green tops)
10 ounces fresh, peeled pearl onions
2 cups chicken broth
1 cup all-purpose flour
¾ cup dry white wine
1 tablespoon butter
1 tablespoon olive oil
1 tablespoon fresh sage
1 tablespoon fresh thyme
½ teaspoon black pepper
½ teaspoon salt

Directions:
1. Melt butter over medium-high heat. Add oil to coat.
2. Sprinkle chicken with salt, pepper, and coat in flour.
3. Place chicken in cooker and brown for about 5 minutes.
4. Add mushrooms and sauté until the liquid evaporates.
5. Remove mushrooms and set aside.
6. Add wine to cooker and once boiling, cook for 30 seconds.

7. Add the chicken, and chicken broth.
8. Secure lid and maintain high pressure for 6 minutes.
9. Quick-release pressure.
10. Add vegetables and bring to high pressure again.
11. As soon as the high pressure is reached, remove from heat and quick-release.
12. With a slotted spoon, move chicken and veggies to a plate.
13. To make the sauce, strain cooking liquid through a cheesecloth. Get rid of any solids.
14. Boil this liquid and reduce for about 12 minutes. Add chopped sage and thyme.
15. Pour over chicken and light some candles!

Nutrition Info (Per Serving):
Calories - 262
Protein - 34.5
Fat - 4
Carbs - 18.5
Fiber - 3.5

Fast Chicken Bouillabaisse
Serves: 4-6
Time: About 10 minutes

We're still in France! A "bouillabaisse" is traditionally a fish stew, but you can make it just as easily (and for less money) with chicken. Sausage and potatoes complement this hearty meal that's perfect for cold winter nights. If you want the bouillabaisse to be especially rich, you can marinate the chicken in the herb-and-oil coating for up to 8 hours beforehand.

Ingredients:
4 chicken thighs
4 Yukon Gold potatoes, peeled and quartered
10-oz of Kielbasa sausage, cut into chunks
1 cup diced tomatoes
½ cup; dry white wine
¾ cup water
½ cup chopped onions
¼ cup chopped celery
¼ cup chopped carrots
1 tablespoon chopped garlic
1 tablespoon olive oil

1 teaspoon grated lemon or orange zest
½ teaspoon saffron threads
¼ teaspoon herbes de Provence
¼ teaspoon pepper
¾ teaspoon salt
½ teaspoon salt

Directions:
1. Mix the oil, saffron, garlic, zest, fennel, salt, pepper herbs, onion, carrots, and celery.
2. Coat chicken in this mixture.
3. Move ingredients to pressure cooker.
4. Add wine, water, potatoes, and tomatoes.
5. Secure lid and bring to highest pressure. Maintain for about 7 minutes on 15 psi.
6. Quick-release the cooker.
7. Add sausage and bring to pressure again for 2 minutes.
8. Quick-release and serve.

Nutrition Info (Per Serving):
Calories - 625
Protein - 68
Fat - 30
Carbs - 11
Fiber - 2

Chicken Pineapple Salad
Serves: 6
Time: 16 minutes

Chicken salad on its own, on a Ritz cracker, or as a sandwich is a tasty, easy lunch or light supper. Making the whole thing in a pressure cooker saves on time and requires very little assembly. This take on the deli classic includes pineapple for a little sweetness and almonds for some crunch.

Ingredients:
2 pounds of cubed, boneless chicken breasts
1 pound diced celery
2 cups chicken broth
2 cups mayo (you can also use plain Greek yogurt if desired)
1 cup toasted almonds, slivered
1 cup pineapple chunks

1 quartered onion
1 bunch diced scallions
1 diced carrot
¼ cup chopped parsley
1 tablespoon lemon juice
1 bay leaf
1 teaspoon curry

Directions:
1. Add chicken, onion, water, ½ cup celery, parsley, and carrot into the pressure cooker.
2. Secure lid and cook at 15 psi for 16 minutes.
3. Quick-release the pressure.
4. Remove chicken and cool.
5. Mix in the rest of the celery, almonds, scallions, and pineapple.
6. In a separate bowl, blend mayo, lemon juice, and curry.
7. Mix with the chicken.
8. Eat warm or cool in the fridge.

Nutrition Info (Per Serving):
Calories - 187
Protein - 23
Fat - 6
Carbs - 14
Fiber - 3

Spanish Chicken Fajitas
Serves: 4
Time: 5 minutes

This fajita recipe is extremely fast. Unique ingredients like raisins and cinnamon add sweetness to the expected kick from the chilies and pepper, while using corn tortillas keeps it all gluten-free. If you're busy and want to spend as little time cooking as possible, this is a perfect weekday meal!

Ingredients:
1 pound boneless, skinless chicken breasts
8 corn tortillas
2 chopped onions, large
1 can diced tomatoes
8 minced garlic cloves

1 sweet red pepper, cut into strips
Another sweet red pepper, chopped
1 mild chili pepper, chopped
1 cinnamon stick
½ cup raisins
1 tablespoon oil
Optional add-ins: Red pepper flakes, beans, shredded cheese

Directions:
1. Heat oil in pressure cooker.
2. Sauté onions, chicken, and garlic until chicken is browned.
3. Add tomatoes, peppers, raisins, and cinnamon.
4. Secure lid and maintain 15 psi for 5 minutes.
5. Remove from heat and let pressure drop naturally for 5 minutes.
6. Remove the rest of the pressure using quick-release.
7. Serve chicken fajita mixture with corn tortillas and optional add-ins.

Nutrition Info (Per Serving):
Calories - 330
Protein - 21
Fat - 11
Carbs - 23
Fiber - 2

Spicy Sriracha-Honey Chicken
Serves: 4
Time: About 10 minutes

If you've been intimidated by some of the ingredient lists thus far, you'll be happy to know that this sweet-and-hot chicken recipe uses items you probably have in your kitchen right now, like ketchup and garlic powder. A dash of Sriracha sauce heats up the sweetness from the honey, and when served with broccoli and rice, this is a tasty dish everyone will love.

Ingredients:
3 pounds skinless, boneless chicken thighs
¾ cup ketchup
¾ cup soy sauce
¾ cup honey
2 tablespoons cornstarch

2 tablespoons water
1 tablespoon chopped basil
1 teaspoon Sriracha sauce
½ teaspoon garlic powder

Directions:
1. Add ketchup, honey, garlic, Sriracha, and soy sauce. Mix.
2. Add chicken.
3. Secure lid and cook until high pressure is reached (about 10 minutes).
4. Use quick-release.
5. In a separate bowl, mix cornstarch with water until dissolved.
6. Mix into pot and simmer until the sauce boils.
7. Add basil.
8. Serve with rice, broccoli, or the veggie of your choice.

Nutrition Info (Per Serving):
Calories - 321
Protein - 36
Fat - 2
Carbs - 19
Fiber - 0

Lime-Salsa Mozzarella Chicken
Serves: 4
Time: 12-15 minutes

Using just salsa and mozzarella, you can transform boring chicken into cheesy, Southwestern deliciousness that's perfect for the summer. Another great thing about this recipe: you can use frozen chicken breasts. If you want to cut the cooking time in half, you can use thawed breasts and cook for only 6 minutes.

Ingredients:
4 skinless, boneless chicken breasts
1 cup salsa
1 cup tomato sauce
1 cup grated Mozzarella cheese
Juice of 2 limes
½ teaspoon salt
¼ teaspoon pepper

Directions:
1. Add chicken, sauce, salsa, salt, pepper, and lime juice to pressure cooker.
2. Secure lid and cook on high pressure for 12 minutes.
3. Quick-release.
4. Remove chicken and place in an oven-safe dish.
5. Cook sauce a little longer until you're pleased with the consistency.
6. Spoon sauce over chicken, and top with cheese.
7. Broil in the oven for about 5 minutes, or until the cheese is melted.
8. Serve with a side of Mexican rice or veggies!

Nutrition Info (Per Serving):
Calories - 295
Protein - 34
Fat - 6
Carbs - 11
Fiber - 0

Thai Peanut Chicken Thighs
Serves: 3-4
Time: 10 minutes

We're heading back to Asia! This time, it's Thailand. Flavorful ingredients like natural peanut butter, ginger, and red pepper flakes cook up with cheap chicken thighs for a convenient weekday supper. If you used a slow cooker, this sort of recipe would take 4-6 hours, but when you use a pressure cooker, everything is ready and on the table in about 10 minutes.

Ingredients:
8 chicken thighs
½ cup chicken broth
¼ cup soy sauce
¼ cup natural peanut butter
¼ cup chopped peanuts (unsalted)
2 tablespoons lime juice
1 tablespoon dried cilantro
1 tablespoon ground ginger
1-2 tablespoons oil
1 tablespoon cornstarch
Red pepper flakes, to taste

Salt and pepper, to taste
Chopped green onions, for garnish

Directions:
1. If using an electric pressure cooker, heat 1 tablespoon oil on the "Browning" setting. If using a stove top, just heat on low.
2. When the oil is nice and hot, brown the meat and set aside on a plate.
3. Mix broth, soy sauce, cilantro, lime juice, ginger, peanut butter, and red pepper in pressure cooker.
4. Add chicken back to pot.
5. Secure lid and cook until high pressure is reached.
6. Quick-release before removing just the chicken, leaving the sauce.
7. In a separate bowl, whisk 2 tablespoons of water and cornstarch until dissolved.
8. Add to pot.
9. Bring to a boil on "Simmer."
10. When thickened, pour over chicken thighs and garnish with green onions and peanuts.

Nutrition Info (Per Serving):
Calories - 363
Protein - 36.2
Fat - 21.7
Carbs - 7.7
Fiber - 2.1

Chicken Cacciatore
Serves: 2-3 people
Time: About 20 minutes

This "hunter's stew" originated in Italy, and warms up cold winter nights. If you want a richer stew, use white wine instead of chicken broth. Rustic herbs like oregano and a single bay leaf add lightly-peppery and aromatic depths. Like most stews, the flavors get richer the next few days after cooking.

Ingredients:
2 pounds boneless, skinless chicken thighs
1 minced onion
2 diced green bell peppers
1 28-ounce can tomatoes

3 minced garlic cloves
¼ cup chicken broth (or white wine)
2 tablespoons olive oil
1 teaspoon dried oregano
1 bay leaf
¼ teaspoon red pepper flakes
Salt and pepper to taste

Directions:
1. Heat olive oil in pressure cooker.
2. Season chicken with salt and pepper.
3. Brown chicken in oil and move to a plate.
4. Next, add the onion and sauté for about 4 minutes.
5. Add garlic, red pepper flakes, and oregano for 1 minute before adding the bay leaf, broth, and tomatoes.
6. Return chicken to pressure cooker and mix.
7. Secure lid, get to high pressure, and maintain for 10 minutes.
8. Quick-release.
9. Add green peppers, bring to high pressure again, and cook for 2 minutes.
10. Quick-release and take out the bay leaf.
11. Season to taste and serve with rice or pasta.

Nutrition Info (Per Serving):
Calories - 239
Protein -34
Fat - 6
Carbs - 11
Fiber - 2.6

Chapter 9 - Beef Entrees

Pressure Cooker Pot Roast

Serves: 4
Time: 1 ½ hours

This classic pot roast recipe cooks up extremely fast in the pressure cooker. While a normal pot roast would take well over three hours, this recipe cuts that down to one and a half hours. Basic ingredients like oil, an onion, and a bay leaf create a delicious gravy to accompany this meal, so it's table-ready.

Ingredients:
3 ½ beef chuck or rump roast
1 chopped onion
1 ½ cups beef broth
2 bay leaves
1 tablespoon vegetable oil
Cornstarch

Directions:
1. Prepare roast by patting dry and seasoning.
2. Heat oil in a pressure cooker.
3. Brown meat on both sides.
4. Remove meat and cook onions and bay leaves in the water.
5. Add the meat to pot and choose high pressure.
6. When high pressure is reached, cook for one hour.
7. Remove from heat and allow pressure to drop.
8. Plate roast.
9. Strain juices and add back to pot.
10. Thicken with cornstarch to desired gravy thickness.
11. Pour over roast and serve with potatoes and/or mixed veggies like carrots and broccoli.

Nutrition Info (Per Serving):

Calories - 467.7
Protein - 36.6
Fat - 23
Carbs - 30.6
Fiber - 4.3

Asian-Inspired Beef Ribs

Serves: 4-6
Time: 1 hour, 20 minutes

For fall-of-the-bone, melt-in-your-mouth ribs. The pressure cooker is one of the best cooking methods you can find. Using some easy-to-find ingredients from the Asian (sometimes called "Exotic" or "Ethnic") section of your grocery store, you can turn some beef ribs into a succulent dinner that's a great alternative to grilling.

Ingredients:
8 beef ribs, cut in half
⅔ cup soy sauce
2 smashed garlic cloves
⅔ cup beef stock
⅔ cup soy sauce
¼ cup rice vinegar
⅓ cup sugar
1 piece of chopped ginger
2 tablespoons cornstarch
1-2 tablespoons water
1 tablespoon sesame oil
Dash of red pepper flakes

Directions:
1. Sauté garlic, sesame oil, ginger, and red pepper flakes in pressure cooker.
2. Mix vinegar, sugar, soy sauce, and beef stock.
3. Add ribs and coat.
4. Secure lid and cook on lowest pressure for 45-60 minutes.
5. Remove from heat and allow pressure to drop naturally.
6. When dropped, remove ribs and brown in your broiler for 5 minutes.
7. Meanwhile, mix cornstarch and water in a separate container.
8. Add to mixture in the pressure cooker and let it boil.
9. Pour over ribs.

Nutrition Info (Per Serving):
Calories - 400
Protein - 26
Fat - 22
Carbs - 24

Corned Beef 'n Cabbage
Serves: 6
Time: About an hour

If you have Irish ancestry or just love an Irish person, you've probably had corned beef and cabbage. This pub favorite also features hearty potatoes and carrots for a one-pot meal perfect for Saint Patrick's Day.

Ingredients:
3 pounds flat-cut, corned beef brisket
One seasoning packet from the corned beef package
8 cloves garlic
4 cups beef broth
6 medium potatoes, quartered (red is best)
3 carrots, cut into pieces
1 quartered onion
1 small cabbage, in 6 wedges

Directions:
1. Rinse the beef.
2. Add broth, onion, garlic, and seasoning packet to pressure cooker.
3. Using the rack attachment, place corned beef in pressure cooker.
4. Secure lid and select high pressure on the electric pressure cooker. Cook for 90 minutes.
5. Remove from heat and let pressure drop naturally for 10 minutes.
6. Quick-release.
7. Remove rack and beef.
8. Add veggies and select High Pressure again.
9. Cook for 3 minutes.
10. Quick-release.
11. When pressure has dropped, plate and serve!

Nutrition Info (Per Serving/2 Cups):
Calories - 304
Protein - 19
Fat - 17.3
Carbs - 21.5

Fiber - 3.8

Mongolian Beef
Serves: 6
Time: 12 minutes

This sweet-and-gingery beef recipe is popular at various Asian restaurants, but when you make it at home, it's less salty and goes great with steamed broccoli and white rice. Using cornstarch helps thicken the sauce, which is my favorite part of this dish.

Ingredients:
2 pounds flank steak
4 pressed garlic cloves
⅔ dark brown sugar
½ cup soy sauce
½ cup water
3 tablespoons water
2 tablespoons cornstarch
1 tablespoon veggie oil
3 green onions, sliced into 1-inch pieces
½ teaspoon minced ginger, fresh

Directions:
1. Season beef with a bit of salt and pepper.
2. Heat oil in an electric pressure cooker and brown meat.
3. Once brown, remove beef, leaving the sauce.
4. Add garlic and choose "sauté.
5. Pour in soy sauce, ½ cup water, ginger, and brown sugar.
6. Add beef back to pressure cooker.
7. Select High Pressure and set timer for 12 minutes. If you're using a stove top pressure cooker, the time is about the same, though you should keep the burner on low to maintain pressure.
8. Quick-release.
9. When ready, combine 3 tablespoons of water and cornstarch in a separate container.
10. Add thickener to pot.
11. Bring to a boil.
12. Add green onions.
13. Serve with veggies and rice.

Nutrition Info (Per Serving/Just meat):

Calories - 360
Protein - 19
Fat - 14
Carbs - 44
Fiber - 0

Shredded Flank Steak
Serves: 2-4 people
Time: 20 minutes

Shredded flank steak is tender and versatile. You can roll it in a burrito, a fajita, or make a sandwich with additional fixings like lettuce, tomato, and hot sauce. When you use a pressure cooker, two pounds of steak cook up in 20 minutes!

Ingredients:
2 pounds flank steak
1 cup chicken broth
1 large onion, cut into quarters
4 minced garlic cloves
Pinch of sea salt

Directions:
1. Season steak with salt.
2. Put steak, onion, broth, and garlic into your pressure cooker.
3. Over medium-high heat, bring broth to a boil.
4. Once that's boiling, secure lid.
5. Cook on high pressure for 20 minutes.
6. Quick-release.
7. When pressure is down, remove the steak.
8. Shred the beef.
9. Season and serve however you want!

Nutrition Info (Per Serving):
Calories - 449
Protein - 57.2
Fat - 21.9
Carbs - 1
Fiber - 0

Beef Stroganoff
Serves: 6
Time: 40 minutes

Beef stroganoff is another meal that usually takes forever. You have to take hours out of your day to prepare it, making it a meal reserved for weekends or holidays. With a pressure cooker, this hearty dish takes less than an hour.

Ingredients:
1 ½ pounds lean beef, cut into 1-inch chunks
12 ounces whole-wheat egg noodles
3 carrots
2 celery stalks, chopped
1 pound white button mushrooms
1 cup dry white wine
1 cup beef broth
1 chopped onion
¼ cup neufchâtel cheese
¼ cup chopped fresh parsley
1 tablespoon flour
1 tablespoon Dijon mustard
1 tablespoon olive oil
Salt and pepper to taste

Directions:
1. Season beef with salt and pepper.
2. In a pressure cooker, heat oil.
3. Add the beef and brown on all sides. This should take about 4 minutes.
4. Add onions and stir, until they are soft and golden.
5. Mix in white wine, flour, and mustard.
6. Simmer until half-reduced in about 2 minutes.
7. Pour in broth, mushrooms, celery, and carrots.
8. Secure lid.
9. Once high pressure is reached, cook for 18 minutes.
10. Quick-release pressure before adding cheese, parsley, pepper, and salt.
11. In another pot, cook the egg noodles.
12. Serve beef with noodles.

Nutrition Info (Per Serving):
Calories - 335
Protein - 29
Fat - 18.4
Carbs - 22.6

Fiber – 20

Quick Beef Tips
Serves: 4-6
Time: 25-30 minutes

For when you want steak, but want something a little different than a big slab of meat. By cubing sirloin steaks and cooking in the pressure cooker, you create mouthwatering, beefy nuggets flavored with onion and spiced with paprika. Serve with the cooked rice of your choice.

Ingredients:
2 pounds top sirloin steak, cubed
2 chopped onions
2 minced garlic cloves
1 can beef consommé
3 tablespoons flour
2 tablespoons vegetable oil
2 teaspoons salt
½ teaspoon black pepper
½ teaspoon paprika
¼ teaspoon mustard powder

Directions:
1. In a Ziploc bag, shake flour, oil, salt, pepper, paprika, and mustard powder until blend.
2. Add beef cubes and coat.
3. Heat oil in the pressure cooker.
4. Brown meat.
5. Add garlic and onions and sauté.
6. Once the onions turn clear, pour in the beef consommé and stir.
7. Secure lid and bring to the highest pressure on the stove top. Cook for 25 minutes.
8. Remove from the burner and let the pressure decrease naturally.
9. If the meat isn't quite to your liking yet, keep the lid off and let it simmer until it's perfect!

Nutrition Info (Per Serving/Beef tips only):
Calories - 611
Protein - 55

Fat - 17
Carbs - 5
Fiber - 0

Pressure-Cooker Rib Eye Steak

Serves: 2
Time: About 20 minutes

If you like steak but can't grill to save your life, or can't use a grill because of your housing rules, the pressure cooker is the best way to prepare a thick, juicy rib eye steak. You also cut out a lot of the fat associated with steak because of the health benefits of pressure cooking!

Ingredients:
2 rib eye steaks (at least 2-inches thick)
Your choice of spices and herbs for seasoning (it's hard to go wrong with salt, pepper, garlic powder, and cayenne)
1 ¼ cup broth
1 tablespoon olive oil

Directions:
1. Pat steak dry and season.
2. Coat the pressure cooker with oil and heat.
3. When hot, sear the steaks on both sides. One side takes about 1 minute.
4. Remove the meat.
5. Pour the broth into the pressure cooker, along with any other spices you want, and scrap off any bits of meat that have stuck to the sides.
6. Add the meat back into the pressure cooker and secure the lid.
7. Bring to high pressure and maintain for 10 minutes.
8. When ready, remove the steak and let it rest for 5 minutes before cutting into it.
9. Serve with any variety of side dish to make the meal complete! Some mixed veggies or even just slices of fresh tomato are great, along with brown rice.

Nutrition Info (Per Serving/Steaks only):
Calories - 385
Protein - 20
Fat - 35

Carbs - 0
Fiber - 0

Cheese-Stuffed Hamburgers

Serves: 2
Time: 25 minutes

If there's a better phrase than "cheese-stuffed," I don't know what it is. Making these gooey hamburgers only takes a half hour with a pressure cooker, and you can add as many veggies (like sauteed onions!) as you want without the guilt. You can even skip the bun if you want to keep things gluten-free.

Ingredients:
1 pound ground beef
2 slices of cheese (think beyond cheddar and try smoked Gouda, buttery Muenster, or Stilton, a mild bleu cheese)
1 tablespoon Worcestershire sauce
½ cup water
Garlic powder
Salt
Pepper
Optional toppings: Tomato, sauteed onions, lettuce, pickles, sprouts, avocado

Directions:
1. Using your hands, mix the beef, sauce, pepper, salt, and garlic powder.
2. Form four balls and flatten with a plate.
3. Lay down 1 ounce (or 1 slice per ball) of cheese in the middle of two of the hamburger patties.
4. Squish the non-cheesed patty atop the cheese patty, forming one burger. Seal the edges tightly with your fingers.
5. Pour ½ cup water into the pressure cooker.
6. Using the steam tray attachment for the burgers, put burgers in the pressure cooker.
7. Secure lid and turn heat to high.
8. Once pressure is reached, maintain for 5 minutes.
9. Remove from heat and let the pressure decrease naturally.
10. Carefully take out the steam tray and serve the burgers with any of the optional toppings!

Nutrition Info (Per Serving/Burgers only):

Calories - 519
Protein - 53
Fat - 34
Carbs - 2
Fiber - 1

Classic Meatloaf
Serves: 4
Time: About 20 minutes

Meatloaf is a great mid-week meal that you might remember from your childhood. It's already pretty easy, but thanks to the pressure cooker, it's done even faster.

Ingredients:
2 pounds ground beef
1 beaten egg
1 cup ketchup (or BBQ sauce)
½ cup broth
½ cup bread crumbs
1 diced yellow onion
¼ cup minced onion
¼ cup grated Parmesan
2 teaspoons Worcestershire
1 tablespoon minced garlic
1 tablespoon veggie oil
½ teaspoon dried thyme
1 teaspoon salt
½ teaspoon pepper

Directions:
1. Mix beef, cheese, minced onion, egg, garlic, bread crumbs, garlic, Worcestershire, thyme, salt, and pepper in a bowl.
2. With your hands, form a loaf.
3. Heat oil in the pressure cooker.
4. Sauté diced onion until clear.
5. Add ketchup and stock and stir.
6. Put the meatloaf in the pressure cooker.
7. Secure lid and maintain high pressure for 15 minutes.
8. Remove from heat and let the pressure release naturally for 10 minutes.
9. Quick-release the rest of the pressure.
10. Plate the meatloaf and pour over sauce.

Nutrition Info (Per Serving):
Calories - 578
Protein - 53
Fat - 28
Carbs - 27
Fiber - 1

Beef Pho with Homemade Broth

Serves: 4
Time: About an hour

If you've cooked some meals with your pressure cooker, and you fancy yourself a decent home chef, this is a good dish to challenge yourself with. It isn't that it's overly complicated, it just uses a lot of ingredients and involves making your own bone broth. The results are definitely worth the work, though, and it only takes about an hour.

Ingredients:
3 pounds beef knuckle or marrow
1 pound boneless beef brisket
½ medium to large Fuji apple
1 large onion
2 ounces fresh ginger
3 whole cloves
2 ½ pieces star anise
2 ½ teaspoons sea salt
1 cinnamon stick
1 ½ - 2 tablespoons fish sauce
½ small red onion
2 green onions
12 ounces pad Thai-style noodles
¼ cup chopped cilantro
Black pepper

Directions:
1. Begin by making the broth. Prepare ingredients by rinsing the bones and beef, peeling and cutting the apple, slicing the onion, and peeling and smashing ginger.
2. Place the star anise, cloves, and cinnamon in the pressure cooker. Sauté until fragrant.
3. Add onion and ginger.

4. Stir for about a minute.
5. Add 9 cups of water.
6. Add beef, apple, bones, and salt.
7. Secure the lid and maintain highest pressure (15 psi) for 20 minutes.
8. Remove from heat and let pressure decrease naturally.
9. Move the meat to a bowl with water and soak for 10 minutes.
10. Strain the broth through a cheesecloth. Get rid of any solids.
11. Skim fat from broth, leaving 3 tablespoons.
12. Add salt and fish sauce.
13. Soak dried noodles until flexible like normal noodles. Rinse.
14. Slice the small red onion and soak for 10 minutes.
15. Slice green onions.
16. Reheat the broth in a normal pot.
17. Heat a pot of water to boiling.
18. Using a mesh sieve, dunk the noodles for 15-20 seconds.
19. Divide up the noodles into 4 bowls.
20. Top with beef, onion, green onion, and cilantro.
21. Pour in 2 cups of broth per bowl.

Nutrition Info (Per Serving):
Calories - 429
Protein - 26
Fat - 26
Carbs - 15
Fiber - 4

Beef Osso Bucco
Serves: 6
Time: 1 hour, 10 minutes

Osso Bucco is traditionally made with veal shanks, but those are pretty expensive. By replacing the veal with beef, you save a lot of money, and still get a hardy meal! You still make the gremolata, which is just garlic, parsley, and lemon, and a fantastic sauce created during the cooking process.

Ingredients:
6 beef shank slices (each about 1 ½ - 2 inches thick)
4 crushed garlic cloves
1 minced garlic clove
1 cup chicken stock
1 cup parsley

Zest from one lemon
15-ounce can diced tomatoes
1 diced carrot
1 diced onion
1 diced celery stalk
½ cup white wine
1 tablespoon tomato paste
1 teaspoon dried thyme
1 teaspoon veggie oil
3 teaspoons salt
½ teaspoon pepper
½ teaspoon salt

Directions:
1. Trim the fat from the beef shanks.
2. Season with 3 teaspoons salt and 1 ½ teaspoons pepper.
3. In the pressure cooker, heat 1 teaspoon oil.
4. Sear the beef shanks, 3 minutes per side and remove from cooker.
5. Pour out the oil and fat in the pressure cooker, leaving one tablespoon.
6. Add garlic, tomato paste, thyme, onion, carrot, and celery.
7. Sauté for 5 minutes.
8. Add wine and stock and *deglaze.
9. Put the shanks back in the pot and submerge.
10. Pour tomatoes on top.
11. Secure lid and maintain at high pressure for 30 minutes on a stove top cooker, 36 for an electric.
12. Remove from heat and decrease pressure naturally for 15 minutes.
13. Quick release.
14. Prepare gremolata by mincing parsley, garlic, and lemon zest together.
15. Remove the shanks and pour pressure cooker into a fat separator (you can get these for about $10-$20 at any store where kitchen equipment is sold)
16. After 10 minutes of resting, pour sauce into a serving bowl.
17. Serve with sauce atop beef shank, and then topped with gremolata.

*Deglazing is when you pour a cooking liquid (like wine or stock) into a pot/pan you have cooked in, and scrap off any bits of food that have stuck to the pot/pan.

Nutrition Info (Per Serving):
Calories - 210
Protein - 27
Fat - 6
Carbs - 9
Fiber - 3

Chapter 10 - Seafood Entrees

Coconut Fish Curry
Serves: 6-8
Time: 20 minutes

Delicate fish combines with coconut milk and Indian spices in this unique take on curry. This creamy dish is so good, you'll want to eat it all on its own! No rice necessary!

Ingredients:
About two pounds of fish fillets, cut into bite-size pieces
1 chopped tomato
17-ounces unsweetened coconut milk
6 basil leaves
2 bell peppers, cut into strips
2 garlic cloves
2 onions, cut into strips
2 tablespoons ground cumin
1 tablespoon grated ginger
1 tablespoon ground coriander
½ teaspoon ground turmeric
1 teaspoon chili powder
½ teaspoon ground fenugreek
Salt to taste
Lemon juice

Directions:
1. Heat oil in the pressure cooker and fry basil leaves for 1 minute.
2. Add ginger, garlic, and onion and sauté until softened.
3. Add cumin, turmeric, coriander, chili, and fenugreek.
4. Sauté for 2 minutes.
5. Deglaze with the coconut milk.
6. Add fish, tomatoes, and peppers. Stir so the fish gets all coated.
7. Maintain the lowest pressure for 5 minutes.
8. Use the quick-release.
9. Serve with salt to taste and a squirt of lemon juice.

Nutrition Info (Per Serving):
Calories - 173

Protein - 27
Fat - 3
Carbs - 10
Fiber - 3

Pressure Cooker Shrimp Paella
Serves: 4
Time: 5 minutes

This is one of the fastest meals you can make with a pressure cooker - your family won't believe it's homemade. Shrimps in the shell cook with jasmine rice for only 5 minutes, creating a succulent, buttery dinner that can be served with grated cheese, parsley, and lemon juice.

Ingredients:
1 pound frozen shrimp in the shell
1 ½ cups chicken broth
1 cup jasmine rice
4 minced garlic cloves
Juice of 1 medium lemon
¼ cup butter
¼ cup parsley
1 pinch saffron
Salt to taste
Pepper to taste
Crushed red pepper to taste

Directions:
1. Put everything in the pressure cooker, with the shrimp on top (shells on).
2. Secure lid and cook on high pressure for 5 minutes.
3. Quick-release the pressure.
4. If you want, you can remove the shrimp from their shells before serving.
5. Serve with a squirt of lemon, grated cheese, and/or parsley.

Nutrition Info (Per Serving):
Calories - 173
Protein - 27
Fat - 3
Carbs - 10
Fiber - 3

Steamed Mediterranean Cod
Serves: 4
Time: About 5 minutes

White fish, like cod, is delicate and melts in your mouth. When made in the pressure cooker with Mediterranean ingredients like olives, capers, tomatoes, and garlic, the plain-tasting cod bursts with flavor. Serve with a big, Greek-inspired salad for a complete Mediterranean experience!

Ingredients:
4 cod fillets
1 pound cherry tomatoes, cut in two
1 cup Kalamata olives
2 tablespoons pickled capers
1 bunch of fresh thyme
1 pressed clove garlic
Olive oil
Salt and pepper to taste

Directions:
1. Line a heat-proof bowl with cherry tomatoes.
2. Add thyme.
3. Put the fish fillets on top of the tomatoes and add any remaining tomatoes, the garlic, a bit of olive oil, and salt.
4. Put the dish in the pressure cooker.
5. Secure lid and maintain high pressure for 4-5 minutes.
6. Quick-release the pressure.
7. Plate fish and sprinkle with thyme, olives, capers, pepper, and olive oil.

Nutrition Info (Per Serving):
Calories - 308
Protein - 21
Fat - 18
Carbs - 14
Fiber - 5

Pressure-Cooker Mussels
Serves: 2-3
Time: 15 minutes

Mussels are a special treat and make for a great date-night first course. When you steam these little guys and eat on a bed of baby spinach, onion, and garlic, you create a delicious briny broth that you ladle over the shellfish.

Ingredients:
2 pounds mussels
1 pound baby spinach
1 small head of radicchio, cut into thin strips
1 clove smashed garlic
½ cup white wine
½ cup water
1 white chopped onion
Olive oil

Directions:
1. Remove the "beard" of the mussels and scrub the shells.
2. Heat olive oil in the pressure cooker.
3. Add onion and garlic.
4. Deglaze with wine and add the steamer basket with the mussels inside.
5. Secure lid and cook on low pressure for 1 minute.
6. Quick-release.
7. Prepare bowls with a bed of baby spinach and radicchio strips.
8. Divide up mussels and pour over broth.

Nutrition Info (Per Serving):
Calories - 303
Protein - 34
Fat - 5
Carbs - 17
Fiber - 10

Pressure-Cooker Lobster Tails
Serves: 3-4
Time: 3 minutes

Lobster is decadent and seems intimidating, but when you cook it in the pressure cooker, it's just 5 minutes and two other ingredients, one of which is water. How easy is that!

Ingredients:

1-2 lbs of lobster tails
1 cup water
¼ cup melted butter (for dipping)
Salt to taste

Directions:
1. Pour water into pressure cooker.
2. Prepare lobster tails by cutting them open from top to tail.
3. Place the lobsters, flesh side up, in the steamer basket.
4. Secure lid and bring to low pressure.
5. Maintain for 3 minutes.
6. Quick-release pressure.
7. Carefully remove lobster tails and serve with melted butter and salt.

Nutrition Info (Per Serving):
Calories - 406
Protein - 57
Fat - 18
Carbs - 3
Fiber - 0

Steamed Crab Legs
Serves: 4
Time: 2 minutes

Crab legs are cheaper than lobster, but just as tasty, especially with lemon butter. Crab can be served on its own, or with fluffy rice pilaf and salad.

Ingredients:
2 lbs frozen crab legs
¾ cup water
4 tablespoons butter
Lemon juice

Directions:
1. Pour ¾ cup water into the pressure cooker.
2. Place crab legs in the steamer basket.
3. Secure lid and cook on highest pressure (15 psi) for 2 minutes.
4. When time is up, the crab legs should be bright pink.

5.   To make the lemon butter, melt butter and combine with juice.
6.   Serve and dip!

Nutrition Info (Per Serving):
Calories - 187
Protein - 16
Fat - 13
Carbs - 0
Fiber - 0

Seafood Gumbo
Serves: 10
Time: About 25 minutes

Louisiana is the birthplace of gumbo, and this recipe uses all the traditional spices and ingredients, like hot Italian sausage, cayenne, and tons of seafood like crab, oysters, and crawfish. Without a pressure cooker, gumbo could take up to three hours, but this version takes less than a half hour!

Ingredients:
1 pound hot Italian sausage
2 quarts chicken stock
½ lump crab meat
2 dozen shucked oysters
2 dozen cooked crawfish tails
4 minced garlic cloves
6 plum tomatoes (peeled, seeded, diced)
1 cup diced white onions
1 cup diced green bell pepper
3 bay leaves
1 ¼ cups flour
¾ cup vegetable oil
½ cup diced celery
2 tablespoons peanut oil
1 teaspoon cayenne pepper
1 teaspoon crushed dried thyme
1 teaspoon paprika
1 teaspoon celery seeds
½ teaspoon garlic powder
½ teaspoon onion powder
Salt and pepper to taste

Directions:
1. To make the roux, combine the veggie oil with flour in a skillet.
   Keep stirring until it turns dark brown and smells nutty.
2. Sauté peppers, celery, onions, and garlic in the pressure cooker, using
3. peanut oil as the coating.
4. After 10-15 minutes, add spices, sausage, chicken stock, and tomatoes.
5. Slowly add ⅔-1 cup of roux to the pressure cooker, one tablespoon at a time.
6. When the mixture is at the desired thickness, add the seafood.
7. Secure lid and maintain high pressure for 10 minutes.
8. Use the cold water method to reduce pressure.
9. Serve!

Nutrition Info (Per Serving):
Calories - 822
Protein - 36
Fat - 58
Carbs - 35
Fiber - 1

Pressure-Cooker Creole Cod
Serves: 8
Time: 5-10 minutes

Cod is a beautiful white fish high in protein and low in calories. This recipe brightens up frozen fillets with ingredients like white wine, garlic, and bay leaves, and makes things a little bit spicy with paprika and cayenne. When served with rice, this easy fish dinner makes a perfect weekday meal when you're in a rush.

Ingredients:
2 packages of frozen cod fillets (2 pounds total)
2 cups chopped onion
2 bay leaves
2 minced garlic cloves
1 chopped green pepper
1 cup chopped celery
1 can tomatoes (28-ounces)

¼ cup white wine
¼ cup olive oil
1 tablespoon paprika
½ teaspoon cayenne pepper
Salt to taste

Directions:
1. Heat olive oil in a pressure cooker.
2. Sauté green pepper, celery, garlic, and onion.
3. Take out the veggies and plate.
4. Drain the juice from the can of tomatoes.
5. Pour juice and wine in the pressure cooker.
6. Put the fish in the steamer basket in a crisscross pattern and place in pressure cooker.
7. Secure lid and cook at 15 psi for 5 minutes.
8. Use the cold-water method to cool the pressure cooker.
9. Take out the fish and put the veggies back in the pressure cooker, along with the tomatoes, bay leaves, and seasonings.
10. Break up the fish and return to pressure cooker.
11. Secure lid and cook until 15 psi is reached.
12. Use the cold-water method to cool.
13. Plate the fish in bowls of rice, and pour sauce over your meal.

Nutrition Info (Per Serving):
Calories - 351
Protein - 51
Fat - 12
Carbs - 6
Fiber - 0

Four White-Fish-Lemon Packets
Serves: 4
Time: 40 minutes

By layering thin slices of potato, onion, and white fish fillets in parchment paper before cooking in the pressure cooker, you get absolutely melt-in-your-mouth results. Lemon, parsley, and thyme brighten up the whole package, creating the perfect summer supper.

Ingredients:
4 fillets of white fish (if frozen, they should be thawed and drained first)
1 white onion, shaved into rings

3 potatoes, very thinly sliced
1 sliced lemon
4 sprigs thyme
4 sprigs parsley
Olive oil
Salt and pepper to taste

Directions:
1. Layer ingredients in oven paper in this order: olive oil, potato, salt and pepper, olive oil, fish, salt and pepper, olive oil, herbs, onion, lemons, salt, and olive.
2. Make the other three packets.
3. Fold and wrap packets in tin foil.
4. Pour two cups of water in pressure cooker.
5. Place two packets in the steamer basket.
6. Secure lid and maintain high pressure for 12-15 minutes.
7. Quick-release.
8. Leave the lid on and wait 5 minutes.
9. Slide packets unto plates.
10. Cook the other two fish packets the same way.
11. Serve and enjoy!

Nutrition Info (Per Serving):
Calories - 191
Protein - 27
Fat - 1
Carbs - 17
Fiber - 3

Simple Salmon 'n Veggies
Serves: 2
Time: About 10 minutes

Salmon, in addition to being delicious, is full of omega-3 fats and vitamin B12 which help hair health and provide protection against diseases. This recipe is great if you're on a high-protein diet, and even if you're not, the tasty salmon paired with broccoli and carrots are still great!

Ingredients:
2 salmon fillets with skin-on, at least 1-inch thick and 6-ounces
2 cups fresh chopped broccoli
1 cup fresh baby carrots

1 cup water
Canola oil
3 cloves
1 bay leaf
1 cinnamon stick

Directions:
1. Put the water in a pressure cooker along with a bay leaf, cinnamon stick broken in half, and whole cloves.
2. Brush some oil on the steamer trivet and put in the pressure cooker.
3. Brush salmon with oil, both sides, and, put in the steamer with the skin down. Put the fillets side by side, not on top of one another.
4. Arrange carrots and broccoli around the fish.
5. Secure the lid and set the pressure to high. Maintain for 6 minutes on an electric pressure cooker.
6. When ready, remove from heat and let the pressure decrease naturally for 4 minutes.
7. Quick-release the rest.
8. Serve fish and veggies with rice or as is!

Nutrition Info (Per Serving):
Calories - 347
Protein - 31
Fat - 19
Carbs - 11
Fiber - 6

Tasty Teriyaki Salmon
Serves: 4
Time: 5 minutes

Teriyaki and salmon go great together! There's something about sweet rice wine, sesame oil, and snappy spring onions that pair perfectly with the creamy, tender fish. Serve on its own, or with rice or soba noodles.

Ingredients:
4-5 pieces of fresh salmon
About 2 ounces of dried mushrooms
1 ½ cups boiling water
¼ cup soy sauce

4 bok choy, washed and cut in half
3 spring onions, cut in half
2 tablespoons sweet rice wine
1 tablespoon caster sugar
1 teaspoon sesame oil

Directions:
1. Pour boiling water over the dried mushrooms.
2. Put the bok choy on the bottom of the pressure cooker. It's okay if you have to layer.
3. Add everything else (including the water and mushrooms) except the salmon.
4. Layer the salmon on top of the bok choy.
5. Cook on high pressure for 4 minutes.
6. Quick-release if you like the salmon a little raw in the middle. If not, let the pressure decrease naturally.

Nutrition Info (Per Serving):
Calories - 393
Protein - 33
Fat - 20
Carbs - 23
Fiber - 0

Pressure-Cooker Salmon Risotto
Serves: 4
Time: 30 minutes

Risotto with salmon is basically savory porridge. It's cooked in chicken broth and white wine, infusing every ingredient with flavor. Throw in some peas and bright lemon peel, and you have a dinner so delicious you'll want to eat the leftovers in the morning.

Ingredients:
1 pound skinless salmon fillets
2 cups Arborio rice
2 cans of chicken broth
½ cup white wine
¾ cup water
1 medium onion
1 cup frozen peas
1 ½ teaspoons grated lemon peel
1 teaspoon olive oil

Salt and pepper to taste

Directions:
1. Heat oil in a pressure cooker.
2. Sauté onion for about 5 minutes.
3. Add rice and stir for 2 minutes.
4. Add wine and cook for 30 seconds until evaporated.
5. Stir in water, broth, salt, and pepper.
6. Secure lid and maintain high pressure for 6 minutes.
7. Quick-release.
8. Take off the cover and mix in peas, salmon, and lemon peel.
9. Cover and let the salmon cook, for about five minutes, in the still-hot pot.

Nutrition Info (Per Serving):
Calories - 414
Protein - 30
Fat - 4
Carbs - 61
Fiber - 6

Chapter 11 - Soups

Classic Chicken Noodle Soup
Serves: 6-8
Time: 21 minutes

When you're sick or it's just a cold winter's night, nothing tastes as good as chicken noodle soup. This version is thickened with savory winter squash and full of tender chicken, onions, celery, and carrots.

Ingredients:
6 cups water
5-8 ounces of egg noodles
2-3 chicken breasts
1-2 cups chopped onions
2 cups diced carrots
2 cups diced celery
2 cups cooked, pureed winter squash
2 cans cream of chicken
3 teaspoons instant chicken bouillon
1 teaspoon celery seed
1 teaspoon onion salt
Parsley
Salt and pepper to taste

Directions:
1. Leaving out the noodles and cream of chicken soup, mix everything in the pressure cooker.
2. Maintain high pressure for 21 minutes.
3. Quick-release.
4. Remove chicken and chop up the meat.
5. Return to the pot and pour in the cream of chicken soups.
6. Heat with the lid off and stir.
7. Cook the egg noodles separately.
8. When cooked, drain and pour into soup.
9. Season with salt and pepper.

Nutrition Info (Per Serving):
Calories - 301
Protein - 21
Fat - 13
Carbs - 23

Fiber - 0

Cheesy Broccoli Soup
Serves: 8-10
Time: 15 minutes

If you have someone in your family who can't stand broccoli, they'll be singing a different tune with this cheesy soup. Break out the blender, and you get a super smooth puree that is great for days to come.

Ingredients:
5 cups of chopped broccoli
5 cups chicken broth
2 cups shredded cheddar
3 teaspoons butter
1 ½ cups of milk
1 chopped garlic clove
Salt and pepper

Directions:
1.   Melt the butter and sauté the garlic until brown and fragrant.
2.   Add the broth and broccoli.
3.   Secure lid and cook for 15 minutes. If using an electric pressure cooker, select the "Soup" setting.
4.   Quick-release the pressure.
5.   If you have a hand blender, puree the soup right in the pressure cooker. If not, pour into a blender.
6.   When smooth, add milk and cheese.
7.   Stir until the cheese is melted.
8.   Serve as is or with a crusty piece of whole-grain bread.

Nutrition Info (Per Serving):
Calories - 261
Protein - 17
Fat - 17
Carbs - 10
Fiber -2

Clam Chowder
Serves: 4-6
Time: 15 minutes

If you don't live on the East Coast, it's hard to find a good clam chowder, and the chowder in cans is usually packed with salt and fat. Making your own chowder is really easy when you use a pressure cooker, and only takes 15 minutes.

Ingredients:
12-24 fresh clams
2 cups clam juice
1 cup smoked bacon
1 cup milk
1 cup cream
1 onion, finely chopped
½ cup tarty white wine
2 medium cubed potatoes (skin on)
1 bay leaf
1 sprig thyme
1 pinch red pepper flakes
1 tablespoon butter
1 tablespoon flour

Directions:

1. Add bacon to the pressure cooker and cook until the fat coats the bottom.
2. Add onion, salt, and pepper and sauté.
3. Add the wine and deglaze the pot.
4. Once the wine evaporates, add the potatoes, clam juice, thyme, bay leaf, and cayenne pepper.
5. Secure the lid and maintain high pressure for 5 minutes.
6. While this is cooking, make the roux by stirring the butter and flour together in a skillet over low heat.
7. Quick-release the pressure cooker and add the clams, cream, milk, and roux.
8. Stir and simmer with the top off for 5 minutes.
9. You can serve the chowder with oyster crackers for texture.

Nutrition Info (Per Serving):
Calories - 265
Protein - 16
Fat - 14
Carbs - 20
Fiber - 6

Pressure-Cooker Ramen
Serves: 8
Time: 90 minutes

When you hear "ramen," you probably think of the freeze-dried noodle packet that keeps college students alive. However, true ramen is a delicious broth-based soup with ginger, pork, chicken, and other toppings of your choice, like hard-boiled eggs, bamboo shoots, and so on.

Ingredients:
1 ½ pounds chicken wings
2 ½ pounds pork spareribs (cut in 2-inch pieces)
3 smashed garlic cloves
2 sliced onions
Ginger nub (about the size of your thumb)
2 tablespoons cooking oil
Water
Soy sauce to taste
Optional toppings: Minced scallions, bean sprouts, cooked bamboo shoots, seaweed, sesame seeds,

Directions:
1. Boil water in a big stockpot. An electric pressure cooker can't get hot enough, but if you have a stove top one, you can use this to boil water.
2. Add the ribs and wings.
3. Return to a boil and let the meat boil for 5-8 minutes.
4. Throw out the water and rinse the meat.
5. Heat oil and sauté the onions for 8 minutes.
6. Add the ginger and garlic, then the meat.
7. Fill the pot with water up to the "max" line.
8. Secure lid and cook on high pressure for 90 minutes.
9. Remove pot from heat and release pressure naturally.
10. Strain through a fine-mesh and throw out any solids.
11. If you want, you can skim off a little fat and oil from the top.
12. You should have a flavorful, dark broth that when refrigerated, becomes like jello.
13. Season with soy sauce and add any toppings.

Nutrition Info (Per Serving):
Calories - 552
Protein - 18

Fat - 20
Carbs - 75
Fiber - 2

Garden Minestrone
Serves: 6
Time: About 20 minutes

Garden minestrone is a fantastic way to use fresh, in-season vegetables. This pressure-cooker soup is loaded with carrots, celery, corn, and more, along with some ditalini pasta to make the soup a bit more filling.

Ingredients:
3 pounds chopped, peeled, and seeded tomatoes
2 large diced carrots
2 cans chicken broth
2 cups baby spinach
1 cup uncooked ditalini pasta
1 14.5-oz can kidney beans
1 diced celery stalk
1 chopped onion
1 chopped zucchini
1 cup fresh corn kernels
1 cup grated Asiago cheese
4 minced garlic cloves
2 tablespoons chopped fresh basil
1 tablespoon olive oil
1 teaspoon Italian seasoning
½ teaspoon black pepper

Directions:
1. Heat olive oil in the pressure cooker.
2. Add onion and sauté for 5 minutes.
3. Add garlic, celery, carrots, corn, zucchini, and garlic. Cook for another 5 minutes.
4. Add chicken broth, pasta, Italian seasoning, salt, and tomatoes.
5. Secure lid and cook on High Pressure for 4 minutes.
6. When done, wait 5 minutes.
7. Quick-release.
8. Add spinach, basil, and beans.
9. Stir and season if necessary.

10. Serve with cheese sprinkled on top.

Nutrition Info (Per Serving):
Calories - 260
Protein - 15
Fat - 8
Carbs - 37
Fiber - 10

Chicken, Chorizo, and Kale Soup
Serves: 8
Time: 10 minutes

Tender chicken thighs and spicy, smoky Chorizo sausage form the meaty base for this rich soup. It's a great option when you're a little sick of the usual veggie-and-meat soups, but don't want to get too adventurous. The addition of chickpeas and kale make things a bit more interesting and healthy!

Ingredients:
9-ounces of pork chorizo, with the casing removed
5-ounces baby kale
4 diced boneless, skinless chicken thighs
4 chopped garlic cloves
4 cups chicken broth
3 peeled, diced medium Yukon gold potatoes
2 chopped onions
2 tablespoons olive oil
2 bay leaves
1 15-oz can diced tomatoes
1 15-oz can chickpeas, drained and rinsed
Salt and pepper to taste

Directions:
1. Heat 2 tablespoons olive oil in the pressure cooker.
2. Add chicken, chorizo, and onion.
3. After 5 minutes, add garlic and cook for another minute.
4. Add broth, bay leaves, and tomatoes. Stir.
5. Add kale and potatoes.
6. Secure lid and cook on High Pressure for 4 minutes.
7. Quick-release pressure.
8. Pick out the bay leaves.
9. Add chickpeas.

10. Season to taste.
11. If the potatoes aren't quite done, sauté.

Nutrition Info (Per Serving):
Calories - 330
Protein - 19
Fat - 20
Carbs - 17
Fiber - 4

Creamy Butternut Squash and Ginger Soup
Serves: 4
Time: 25 minutes

If you haven't been using butternut squash when it's in-season, you are majorly missing out. Butternut squash is packed with antioxidants, vitamin A, and it's a fantastic vegetable for people who don't like vegetables. When it's pureed in a soup, it's like eating cream, and just a little ginger cuts some of the veggie's natural sweetness.

Ingredients:
4 pounds peeled, seeded, and cubed butternut squash
4 cups veggie stock
1 chopped onion
Fresh ginger, peeled, and sliced
¼ teaspoon nutmeg
1 sprig of sage
Olive oil
Salt and pepper to taste

Directions:
1. Sauté onions in the pressure cooker with salt, pepper, and sage in a little oil.
2. Once onions are softened, add enough squash to cover the bottom of the pressure cooker. Just move the onions around a bit.
3. Brown for 10 minutes.
4. Add the rest of the squash and the ginger, stock, and nutmeg.
5. Secure lid and maintain the highest pressure for 15 minutes.
6. Quick-release the pressure.
7. Pick out the sage stem.
8. Blend the soup using a regular blender or hand blender.

9. Serve and enjoy!

Nutrition Info (2 cups per serving):
Calories - 397
Protein - 19
Fat - 8
Carbs - 8
Fiber - 3

Chicken Wild Rice Soup

Serves: 4
Time: 30 minutes

Chicken wild rice soup is a classic deli favorite, and can be whipped up in your pressure cooker in a half hour. Wild rice is arguably the healthiest rice and has more fiber and protein in it than white has, and it's lower in carbs than brown. Combined with chicken, thyme, veggies, and even heavy whipping cream, this creamy soup is delicious and nutritious.

Ingredients:
4 cups chicken stock
1 large chicken breast, cut into cubes
6-ounces sliced mushrooms
1 cup heavy whipping cream
½ cup wild rice
¼ cup dry sherry
2 diced celery stalks
4 diced carrots
2 tablespoons butter
2 tablespoons flour
¼ teaspoon ground thyme
Salt, pepper, and nutmeg to taste

Directions:
1. Pour chicken stock and wild rice in the pressure cooker. Cook on high pressure for 20 minutes.
2. Quick-release pressure and add chicken, carrots, celery, and onion.
3. Cook on high pressure for 3 minutes.
4. In a separate bowl, mix softened butter with flour to make a paste.
5. Add sherry and mushrooms to mixture.

6. Add to pressure cooker and cook uncovered for 3-5 minutes, until mushrooms are cooked through.
7. Add the cream and mix.
8. Season to your liking with nutmeg, salt, and pepper!

Nutrition Info (2 cups per serving):
Calories - 381
Protein - 18
Fat - 21
Carbs - 24
Fiber - 1

Tomato Basil Soup
Serves: 8
Time: 10 minutes

Tomato soup with a grilled cheese sandwich is a classic lunch. This recipe uses shredded Parmesan, so even if you don't have a sandwich with the soup, you get that cheesiness.

Ingredients:
3 pounds tomatoes, cored, peeled, and cut into quarters
2 14.5-ounces cans chicken broth
2 diced celery stalks
1 diced onion
1 diced carrot
3 tablespoons butter
1 cup half & half
½ cup shredded Parmesan cheese
¼ cup fresh basil
1 tablespoon tomato paste
½ teaspoon ground pepper
½ teaspoon salt

Directions:
1. Melt butter in a pressure cooker.
2. Sauté carrots, celery, and onions.
3. When they're tender, add the garlic and cook for 1 minute.
4. Add the chicken stock, basil, tomatoes, salt, and pepper.
5. Cook on high pressure for 5 minutes.
6. When time is up, remove from heat, and wait another 5 minutes.
7. Quick-release the pressure.

8. Puree the soup with a hand blender or a regular one until smooth.
9. While the soup is still warm, stir in the cheese and half & half. If using an electric pressure cooker, select "Simmer."

Nutrition Info (Per Serving):
Calories - 314
Protein - 11
Fat - 23
Carbs - 16
Fiber - 2

French Onion Soup

Serves: 4-5
Time: 11 minutes

This rich, cheesy soup is not low in calories and is definitely not health food, but making it yourself lets you control the unhealthy ingredients, like salt and how much cheese you use. You can even make your own croutons if you want!

Ingredients:
4 cups diced sweet onions (organic is best)
4 cups beef broth
2 garlic cloves, thinly-sliced
½ cup dry sherry
½ cup Gruyere cheese
2 teaspoons dried thyme
1 tablespoon olive oil

Directions:
1. Heat olive oil in a pressure cooker.
2. Sauté garlic and onions.
3. When they're soft, add sherry, 2 cups of broth, and thyme.
4. Secure the lid and cook on high pressure for 8 minutes.
5. Quick-release the pressure.
6. Add the rest of the broth and simmer.
7. Season with salt and pepper.
8. Now it's time to melt the cheese in the broiler. Pour soup into oven-safe bowls.
9. Sprinkle on cheese and put in the broiler for 3 minutes, or until the cheese melts.

To make the croutons:
1. Prepare a slightly-sale loaf of bread by pulling it apart into crouton-like
2. bits.
3. On a baking sheet, drizzle a little olive oil and arrange the bread. Drizzle more on top and toss with salt. Make sure the croutons aren't touching each other.
4. Bake in a 375-degree oven for 5 minutes. Stir the croutons and bake for another 5 minutes or until crunchy.

Nutrition Info (Per Serving/Without Croutons):
Calories - 195
Protein - 8
Fat - 9
Carbs - 16
Fiber - 1

Fast Chicken Stock
Serves: 3-4
Time: 30 minutes

Being able to make your own chicken stock is an absolute must-have skill for any serious home chef. When you pressure cook it, it only takes 30 minutes, and you can use it for just about any recipe.

Ingredients:
1 chicken carcass
10 garlic cloves
15 whole black peppercorns
3-4 liters cold water
1 large carrot
1 large onion
1 celery stalk

Directions:
1. Put the chicken, celery, carrot, onion, garlic, and peppercorns in a pressure cooker.
2. Pour water up to the ⅔ mark.
3. Secure the lid.
4. Maintain high pressure for 30 minutes.
5. Remove from heat and let the pressure decrease naturally.
6. Strain the stock and get rid of all the solids.
7. Cool to room temperature before putting in the fridge.

Calories - 86
Protein - 6
Fat - 3
Carbs - 8
Fiber - 0

Leftover Turkey-and-Veggie Soup

Serves: 6-8
Time: About 90 minutes

This soup is a great way to use up Thanksgiving leftovers, specifically the bones of your turkey. Using the carcass, you create a savory broth that forms a perfect base for onions, egg noodles, turkey meat, and mixed veggies.

Ingredients:
3 quarts of water
Turkey bones (with meat)
2 quarts turkey stock
2 bay leaves
2 cups shredded turkey, cooked
2 cups frozen mixed veggies
1 minced shallot
1 onion, cut in half
1 carrot
1 ½ cups egg noodles
1 tablespoon butter
1 teaspoon fresh thyme
Salt and pepper to taste

Directions:
1. Begin by making the broth. Put the turkey carcass, celery, bay leaves, onion, carrot, and salt in the pressure cooker. Pour in water.
2. Secure lid and maintain high pressure for 50 minutes on the stove top.
3. Let the pressure come down naturally.
4. Remove solids.
5. Plan on using 2 quarts of this stock for the soup.
6. Melt the butter in the pressure cooker.
7. Sauté the shallot and thyme.

8. When brown, add the 2 quarts of turkey stock.
9. Bring to a boil.
10. Add turkey meat, noodles, and mixed veggies.
11. Simmer for 10 minutes or until the noodles are cooked through.
12. Season before serving.

Nutrition Info (Per Serving/One cup):
Calories - 72
Protein - 3
Fat - 3
Carbs - 8.6
Fiber - .5

Chapter 12 - Vegan Entrees

Vegan Chili
Serves: 6-8
Time: 40 minutes

Chili is usually a meat-lover's dish, but this vegetable-packed version is made for vegetarians and vegans. It uses a veggie ground round, which is a meat substitute that improves the flavor of the chili, as well as two kinds of beans and fresh tomatoes. Perfect for cold-weather dinners and lunches!

Ingredients:
1 pack veggie ground round (Yves is a good brand)
About 4 cups water
8 ounces of pinto beans (soak before use)
8 ounces red kidney beans (soak before use)
13 ounces chopped Roma tomatoes
2 chopped onions
3 minced garlic cloves
1 diced bell pepper
1 bay leaf
2 tablespoons olive oil
1 tablespoon chili powder
2 teaspoons cumin
1 ½ teaspoons oregano
Salt to taste

Directions:
1. Heat olive oil in the pressure cooker.
2. Sauté the garlic and onions.
3. Add veggie ground round and brown.
4. Add the bell pepper, chili powder, cumin, oregano, bay leaf, and salt. Mix.
5. Put in the beans, tomatoes, and water. Stir.
6. Secure lid and maintain low pressure for 20 minutes.
7. Remove from heat and let the pressure drop naturally.
8. Pick out the bay leaf.
9. Serve right away.

Nutrition Info (Per Serving):
Calories - 192

Protein - 15
Fat - 6
Carbs - 24
Fiber - 9

Vegan Hot Tamales

Serves: 12-15
Time: 50 minutes

This vegan-friendly tamales recipe makes 36-40 tamales (depending on how big they are), which is enough to feed a hungry crowd. Steaming them in a 5-liter pressure cooker, or one that's larger, lets you work faster. In addition to the must-have masa, vegan fillings include beans, Mexican rice, and cooked veggies.

Ingredients:
2 cups water
1 pack of corn husks
Fillings - rice, re-fried beans, salsa, veggies
3 cups masa harina
1 cup corn oil (or olive oil)
2 teaspoons baking powder
1 teaspoon salt
Chili sauce

Directions:
1. Rinse the corn husks.
2. Arrange them in a casserole dish and pour boiling water over them, so they're covered.
3. In a heavy mixer, combine the masa harina, oil, baking powder, and salt.
4. Pour (very slowly) in about 1 ½ cups of the liquid until a "play-doh" consistency is achieved.
5. Begin to construct the tamales. Flip the tamales so the side that was down in the casserole dish is facing up.
6. Dry with a kitchen towel and spread a layer of masa on the middle ⅔ of the husk.
7. Put a dollop of filling in the middle, topped with chile sauce.
8. Fold and then fold the bottom part, so the tops arc open.
9. Add 2 cups of water to the pressure cooker and steamer basket.
10. Put the tamales in the steamer, but not horizontally.

11. To save space, you can tie three together with kitchen string and stand them up.
12. Secure lid.
13. Maintain high pressure for 15-20 minutes.
14. Let the pressure come down naturally.
15. When the pressure is down, serve in their wrappers!

Nutrition Info (Per Serving):
Calories - 124
Protein - 1.5
Fat - 9
Carbs - 8.6
Fiber - .8

Pulled Jack-Fruit Sandwich
Serves: 4
Time: 6 minutes

This is an incredibly creative vegan recipe. Instead of pulled pork, this sandwich uses jack fruit, which has a meaty texture and is seasoned with vegan Worcestershire, mustard seeds, and sweet maple. When you're buying jack fruit, be sure to get the kind in water, not syrup. You can find canned jack fruit at most Asian markets.

Ingredients:
1 can (17-ounces) jack fruit, drained and rinsed
4 toasted buns
½-¾ cup water
¼ cup diced onion
3 tablespoons tomato paste
1 tablespoon maple syrup
1 tablespoon minced garlic
1 teaspoon olive oil
1 teaspoon apple cider vinegar
1 teaspoon Vegan Worcestershire sauce
½ teaspoon yellow mustard seeds
½ teaspoon cayenne pepper
½ teaspoon salt
½ teaspoon black pepper

Directions:
1. Heat the oil in the pressure cooker.

2. Sauté the onion and garlic until soft.
3. Add all the seasonings, jack fruit, vinegar, syrup, Worcestershire, and tomato paste.
4. Stir.
5. Add water so that the jack fruit is covered. Mix again.
6. Secure lid and maintain high pressure for 3 minutes.
7. Remove from heat and let the pressure decrease naturally.
8. Stir and shred the jack fruit using a fork.
9. Serve on buns with cabbage or other Vegan toppings.

Nutrition Info (Per Serving/With Bun):
Calories - 295
Protein - 7
Fat - 3
Carbs - 62
Fiber - 1

20-Minute Miso Risotto
Serves: 4-6
Time: 20 minutes

Miso is fermented soybean, and is a great addition to foods that usually require meat. It adds a deep, sweet-salty flavor, as well as important vitamins and antioxidants that aid in digestion and preventing disease. It's often used as an add-in to other dishes, but in this risotto, it adds the main flavor and is highlighted by scallions, lemon, and sake.

Ingredients:
4 cups vegetable stock
2 cups Arborio rice
6 tablespoons olive oil
3 minced garlic cloves
¾ cup dry sake
¼ cup white or yellow miso paste
1 minced shallot
2 teaspoons soy sauce
½ teaspoon lemon juice
Salt to taste
Minced scallions

Directions:
1. In a pressure cooker, heat olive oil.

2.   Add the garlic and shallots.
3.   When clear, add the rice.
4.   Stir until the rice is toasted, but not browned. This will take about 3-4 minutes.
5.   Pour in the sake and stir until evaporated.
6.   Add miso and soy sauce.
7.   Deglaze the pot with the stock until all the bits of rice, shallots, and garlic are covered.
8.   Secure the pressure cooker and bring to the lowest pressure (10 psi) and maintain for 5 minutes.
9.   Quick-release pressure.
10. Add the lemon juice and stir.
11. The risotto should be creamy, not watery.
12. Season with salt and sprinkle with chopped scallions.

Nutrition Info (Per Serving/With Bun):
Calories - 569
Protein - 8
Fat - 23
Carbs - 80
Fiber - 1

Pressure-Cooker Feijoada
Serves: 6
Time: 40 minutes

This dish is traditionally a pork-and-beans stew, but to make this vegan, you use a vegan sausage. Other than that, it uses all the same ingredients like black beans, onions, carrots, and soy curls, which help make up for the lack of meat.

Ingredients:
2 ½ cups water
2 cups dried black beans (that have been soaked overnight)
1 spicy vegan sausage, chopped
1 cup soy curls (softened in hot water for 15 minutes and drained)
2 onions, sliced into rings
2 large carrots, cut into ¼-inch disks
1 chopped red bell pepper
4 minced garlic cloves
⅓ cup dry red wine
2 bay leaves
1 tablespoon cumin

½ tablespoon liquid smoke
½ tablespoon paprika
½ tablespoon dried thyme
Ground pepper to taste
Optional Toppings: Cilantro, avocado, onions

Directions:
1. Sauté the carrots, onions, bell pepper, and garlic in a bit of water for 5 minutes.
2. Add cumin, liquid smoke, thyme, pepper, and paprika.
3. Stir for 1 minute and add red wine after another 1-2 minutes.
4. Add the bay leaves, broth, veggie sausage, beans, and soy curls.
5. Secure lid and cook on high pressure for 30 minutes. On an electric cooker, choose the Bean/Chile setting.
6. Let the pressure decrease naturally.
7. The beans should be soft. Serve with optional toppings and enjoy!

Nutrition Info (Per Serving):
Calories - 328
Protein - 20
Fat - 4
Carbs - 54
Fiber - 13

Pressure-Cooker Lentils
Serves: 6
Time: 10-15 minutes

These lentils cooked with chopped tomatoes, onion, and celery, and seasoned with curry and pepper, make a great midday snack or light lunch, if you are vegan. Lentils are packed with protein and have been shown to boost energy levels, which is perfect for the middle of a long work day. If you need a bit more heft to your meals, serve on top of polenta or rice.

Ingredients:
2 cups water
1 ½ cups of chopped tomatoes
1 ½ cups dry lentils
1 medium green pepper
1 chopped onion

1 chopped celery stalk
1 tablespoon extra-virgin olive oil
1 teaspoon curry powder
1 teaspoon salt

Directions:
1. Heat oil in a pressure cooker.
2. Sauté the celery, green pepper, and onion.
3. When soft, add chopped tomatoes and mix.
4. Secure lid and maintain high pressure for 10-15 minutes.
5. Remove from heat and let the pressure decrease naturally.
6. Spoon into bowls and serve!

Nutrition Info (Per Serving):
Calories - 105
Protein - 7
Fat - 3
Carbs - 14
Fiber - 5

Italian Tofu Scramble
Serves: 4
Time: 7 minutes

This quick vegan scramble uses firm tofu as a base instead of eggs, and includes delicious and springy Italian seasoning, onions, carrot, and tomatoes. This is a great breakfast, lunch, dinner, or midnight snack option, and it's one you'll want to make over and over again.

Ingredients:
1 block extra-firm tofu, drained, not pressed
1 small onion, cut into half-moon slices
3 minced garlic cloves
1 cup diced carrot
¼ cup vegetable broth
1 can Italian-style diced tomatoes
2 tablespoons jarred banana pepper rings
1 tablespoon Italian-style seasoning
Italian blend nutritional yeast
1 teaspoon cumin
1 teaspoon walnut oil
Ground black pepper
Directions:

1. Heat oil in an uncovered pressure cooker.
2. Add garlic, carrots, and onion for 3 minutes.
3. Crumble the tofu and add the broth, peppers, cumin, tomatoes, and seasoning.
4. Mix.
5. Secure the lid and maintain high pressure for 4 minutes.
6. Quick-release the pressure.
7. Mix in nutritional yeast and black pepper.
8. Serve and enjoy!

Nutrition Info (Per Serving):
Calories - 144
Protein - 12
Fat - 6
Carbs - 13
Fiber - 3

Pressure-Cooker Seitan with Red Wine Mushroom Sauce
Serves: 4
Time: 25-30 minutes

Seitan is a popular meat substitute that has a chicken-like texture, and is full of protein. This recipe combines the seitan with a truly decadent red wine mushroom sauce and herbs like rosemary and thyme. It's a sophisticated vegan dinner that will impress anyone.

Ingredients:
3 cups vegetable broth
2 cups water
¼ cup aminos
2 tablespoons vegan Worcestershire sauce
1 teaspoon onion powder
1 ½ cups vital wheat gluten
1 cup vegetable broth
⅓ cup tapioca flour
3 tablespoons nutritional yeast
2 tablespoons liquid aminos
1 tablespoon olive oil
1 tablespoon vegan Worcestershire sauce
1 teaspoon garlic powder
½ teaspoon dried rosemary
½ teaspoon dried thyme
¼ teaspoon sea salt

¼ teaspoon black pepper
8-ounces baby bella mushrooms, sliced
⅔ cup red wine
1 minced garlic clove
1 tablespoon coconut oil
1 tablespoon fresh rosemary sprigs
¼ teaspoon sea salt
Black pepper to taste

Directions:
1. To make the seitan, look to the second set of ingredients.
2. Mix the dry ingredients.
3. Mix the wet ingredients separately, and add to the dry ingredients.
4. Fold with a spoon and then knead with your hands for 2-3 minutes.
5. Make a round shape from the seitan, cup in your hands, and pull the dough at the top and roll it under. It will look smooth.
6. Continue forming until it looks oblong. Roll it tightly in a cheesecloth.
7. Close the ends with some string.
8. Put the roast in the pressure cooker.
9. Looking to the first set of ingredients, pour in everything. This makes the simmering broth.
10. Stir and secure the lid to the pressure cooker.
11. Maintain high pressure for 25 minutes.
12. Decrease the pressure immediately by running it under cold water.
13. To make the red wine mushroom sauce, look to the last set of ingredients.
14. Heat the coconut oil in a skillet and sauté garlic for 2 minutes.
15. Add the wine, rosemary, and mushrooms.
16. Once boiling, reduce to a simmer and cook uncovered until the mushrooms have shrunk and the sauce is thicker.
17. Season with sea salt and pepper.
18. Remove the seitan roast and slice.
19. Pour the sauce over the roast and serve.

Nutrition Info (Per Serving):
Calories - 260
Protein - 34

Fat - 7
Carbs - 16
Fiber - 3

Black-Eyed Pea & Collard Green Chili
Serves: 4-6
Time: 15 minutes

There are a lot of ways to do chili, and this vegan-friendly version is full of delicious ingredients like black-eyed peas, red onion, and spices like oregano and cinnamon. Who says vegan food has to be boring?

Ingredients:
4 large collard green leaves
1 28-ounce can diced tomatoes
1 8-ounce can diced tomatoes
2 cups chopped carrots
2 cups chopped celery
2 cups rinsed and drained
2 cups vegetable broth
2 bay leaves
2 cups dried black-eyed peas
3 minced garlic cloves
1 cup water
½ cup diced red onion
1 seeded and diced fresh jalapeno
½ diced red bell pepper
2 tablespoons chili powder
1 tablespoon dried oregano
1 teaspoon cumin
1 teaspoon ground cinnamon
1 teaspoon extra-virgin olive oil
½ teaspoon ground coriander
Sea salt to taste
Chopped green onion for garnish

Directions:
1. Cut each collard leaf lengthwise and get rid of the center ribs.
2. Cut crosswise, so you get strips about 6mm wide.
3. Heat oil in the pressure cooker and sauté onion and garlic for 2 minutes.
4. Add celery and carrots, and cook for 3-5 minutes.

5. Add collard greens, cumin, chili powder, coriander, cinnamon, oregano, and jalapeno.
6. Sauté for a minute or so.
7. Add the water, black-eyed peas, bay leaves, tomatoes, tomato sauce, and broth.
8. Secure lid and cook at high pressure for 10 minutes.
9. Let the pressure decrease naturally.
10. Season to taste. If the peas aren't done yet, let them simmer uncovered for a bit.
11. Pick out the bay leaves before serving.

Nutrition Info (Per Serving):
Calories - 195
Protein - 7
Fat - 1.3
Carbs - 41.5
Fiber - 10.8

Chapter 13 - Side Dishes

Pressure-Cooker Cornbread
Serves: 8
Time: 16 minutes

Homemade cornbread is one of the small pleasures in life. It goes with chili, soups, and by itself served warm with a dab of butter. Making bread in a pressure cooker might seem weird, but it turns out very well, and only takes 16 minutes when you cook on high pressure.

Ingredients:
1 ¼ cups cornmeal (fine, freshly-ground popcorn)
1 cup milk
1 cup white flour
1 big egg
½ cup sugar
¼ cup melted butter
1 tablespoon baking powder
½ teaspoon salt

Directions:
1. Pour 2 cups of water and just a splash of white vinegar to your pressure cooker.
2. Put a metal trivet on the bottom.
3. Prepare a round bread pan (that fits in the pressure cooker) with cooking oil.
4. In a bowl, beat the butter, milk, and egg together.
5. Stir in the other ingredients until the flour is just moist.
6. Pour batter into pan and wrap closed with foil.
7. Cook in pressure cooker for 16 minutes on high pressure.
8. Let the pressure come down naturally before unwrapping and serving.

Nutrition Info (Per Serving):
Calories - 183
Protein - 4
Fat - 6
Carbs - 27
Fiber - 2

Parmesan Prosecco Risotto

Serves: 6
Time: About 10 minutes

This rich, cheesy side dish would pair well with just about any kind of meat. Imagine it with a nice juicy cut of steak, along with fresh green beans. The secret to this dish is the sparkling white wine.

Ingredients:
3 cups chicken broth
1 ⅓ cups uncooked medium-grain rice
3 minced garlic cloves
⅔ cup finely-chopped shallots
1 cup sparkling white wine
2 ounces fresh Parmigiano-Reggiano cheese
1 ½ tablespoons butter
1 teaspoon fresh thyme leaves
½ teaspoon grated lemon rind
¼ teaspoon ground pepper

Directions:
1. Heat butter until melted.
2. Add shallots and sauté for 2 minutes.
3. Add garlic and sauté that, stirring the whole time.
4. Add the rice and cook for 1 minute, still stirring.
5. Add ½ cup sparkling wine and cook until the liquid is absorbed.
6. Add the rest of the wine and broth.
7. Secure lid and maintain high pressure for 8 minutes.
8. Remove from heat and run cold water to release the pressure.
9. Grate cheese and stir in, along with the rest of the ingredients.
10. Let rest for 4 minutes.
11. Top with a few more cheese shavings.

Nutrition Info (¾ cup/Per Serving):
Calories - 239
Protein - 8.8
Fat - 5.9
Carbs - 38.7
Fiber - 2.5

Fast Potato Salad

Serves: 4
Time: 60 minutes

Potato salad is a classic side dish at potlucks and cookouts. This pressure cooker version is a great option for when you only have a few hours to prepare.

Ingredients:
6 medium potatoes, peeled and cut into cubes
4 large eggs
1 ½ cups water
1 cup mayonnaise
2 tablespoons chopped fresh parsley
1 tablespoon pickle juice
1 tablespoon mustard
Salt and pepper

Directions:
1. Add water into pressure cooker.
2. In the steamer basket, add potatoes and eggs.
3. Secure lid and cook on high pressure for 4 minutes.
4. Quick-release.
5. Remove eggs and place in ice water.
6. In another bowl, mix mayo, onion, parsley, pickle juice, and mustard.
7. Add the potatoes and mix.
8. Peel and cut up cooled eggs and add into potato salad.
9. Season with salt and pepper.
10. Chill at least an hour before eating.

Nutrition Info (1 cup/Per Serving):
Calories - 358
Protein - 6.7
Fat - 5.9
Carbs - 20.5
Fiber - 3.3

Quinoa Almond Pilaf

Serves: 4
Time: 11 minutes

With just a few basic ingredients, you can create an easy and unique side dish that's a lot more interesting than plain rice or mixed vegetables. When the onion and celery are sauteed in butter, they become a little sweet, which goes great with the natural nuttiness of the quinoa and almonds.

Ingredients:
1 ½ cups rinsed and drained quinoa
1 finely chopped celery
1 14-ounce chicken broth
½ cup chopped onion
½ cup toasted, sliced almonds
¼ cup water
2 tablespoons chopped parsley
1 tablespoon butter
½ teaspoon salt

Directions:
1. Heat butter in a pressure cooker and sauté chopped celery and onions.
2. Cook for about 3-5 minutes.
3. Add the broth, water, quinoa, and salt.
4. Secure lid and cook on high pressure for 1 minute.
5. Quick-release the pressure.
6. If all the liquid isn't absorbed, steam for a few more minutes.
7. Mix in almonds and parsley.

Nutrition Info (1 cup/Per Serving):
Calories - 210
Protein - 4
Fat - 13
Carbs - 21
Fiber - 3

Spicy Black Bean Brown Rice Salad
Serves: 4-8
Time: 34 minutes

Pressure cookers are so versatile, you can even make salads in them! This healthy side dish combines black beans, brown rice, tomatoes, and avocado with a spicy citrus dressing that brightens and brings the whole thing together.

Ingredients:
1 ½ cups of water
1 (14-ounce) can drained, and rinsed black beans
12 quartered grape tomatoes
1 cup brown rice
1 diced avocado
¼ cup minced cilantro
¼ teaspoon salt
2 minced garlic cloves
3 tablespoons extra-virgin olive oil
3 tablespoons fresh lime juice
2 teaspoons Tabasco
1 teaspoon agave nectar
⅛ teaspoon salt

Directions:
1. Mix water, rice, and salt in the pressure cooker.
2. Secure lid and cook on high pressure for 24 minutes.
3. Let the pressure decrease naturally for 10 minutes, then do a quick-release for the rest.
4. Fluff the rice a little before cooling.
5. If you're eating right away, mix the rice with beans, tomato, avocado, and cilantro.
6. Make the dressing by whisking the Tabasco, garlic, agave, lime juice, and salt. Slowly add the olive oil as you mix.
7. Pour the dressing over the salad and eat up!

Nutrition Info (Per Serving):
Calories - 140
Protein - 3.5
Fat - 2.8
Carbs - 28
Fiber - 2

Roasted Cauliflower Barley Risotto
Serves: 4
Time: 25 minutes

Roasted cauliflower has a beautiful nutty flavor that pairs beautifully with pearl barley and the flavors of thyme, rosemary, and garlic. You can make this risotto vegetarian by replacing the chicken broth with veggie broth, if you need to.

Ingredients:
1 head cauliflower (small is best)
2 cloves minced garlic
3 cups chicken broth
1 diced onion
1 cup pearl barley
3 tablespoons olive oil
½ cup fresh grated Parmesan
2 sprigs thyme
2 tablespoons chopped fresh parsley
1 tablespoon butter

Directions:
1. The cauliflower cooks in the oven. Preheat oven to 426 degrees Fahrenheit and cut the cauliflower into florets.
2. Toss with olive oil and season with salt and pepper.
3. Spread out the florets on a foil-lined baking sheet.
4. Roast for about 20 minutes, tossing halfway through.
5. While the cauliflower roasts, heat 1 tablespoon olive oil in the pressure cooker.
6. Sauté the onion and garlic.
7. Pour in broth, thyme, and barley.
8. Secure lid and cook on high pressure for 25 minutes.
9. The cauliflower should be done by now, so sprinkle with ¼ cup grated Parmesan, and roast for about 5 minutes more, so for a total of 25 minutes in the oven.
10. Quick-release the pressure cooker.
11. Cook uncovered until the barley is tender and the risotto has a porridge-like consistency.
12. Pick up the thyme stems.
13. Add butter and ¼ cup Parmesan and blend.
14. Mix in the cauliflower florets and parsley.
15. Season to taste with salt and pepper, and sprinkle with any remaining cheese.
16. Serve with your choice of protein!

Nutrition Info (Per Serving):
Calories - 295
Protein - 11
Fat - 8
Carbs - 41
Fiber - 10

Pressure-Cooker Cheesy Potatoes

Serves: 4
Time: 12 minutes

Crunchy from the panko and onion, creamy from the sour cream and cheese, these potatoes au gratin are a classic side dish that you'll want to eat for your main dish. This isn't health food, but it's a great treat to go along with a solid protein like steak.

Ingredients:
6 medium potatoes, peeled and sliced ⅛-inch thick
1 cup chicken broth
1 cup cheddar cheese
1 cup panko bread crumbs
3 tablespoons melted butter
½ cup onion
½ cup sour cream
2 tablespoons butter
Salt and pepper to taste

Directions:
1. Sauté 2 tablespoons butter in the pressure cooker.
2. When melted, add onion for 5 minutes.
3. Pour in 1 cup chicken broth, salt, and pepper.
4. Put the sliced potatoes in the steamer basket and cook on high pressure for 5 minutes.
5. Preheat broiler.
6. In a bowl, mix panko with 3 tablespoons of melted butter.
7. Quick-release the pressure cooker.
8. Put the potatoes in a greased 9x13 oven-safe dish.
9. Mix cheese and sour cream into the pressure-cooker liquid and pour over potatoes.
10. Top with the panko/butter mixture.
11. Broil for 5-7 minutes until golden.
12. Serve!

Nutrition Info (Per Serving):
Calories - 150
Protein - 3
Fat - 6
Carbs - 22
Fiber - 1

Whole White Beets with Greens
Serves: 2
Time: 20 minutes (after green-soaking)

White beets are sweeter than regular, red ones, and have less of that fresh-from-the-ground taste. They're lighter, smoother, and come with their own greens.

Ingredients:
3 whole white beets with green tops
2 minced garlic cloves
1 tablespoon olive oil
1 teaspoon salt
1 teaspoon lemon juice

Directions:
1. Cut off the greens and wash.
2. After 30 minutes, leave out the greens and put them in a strainer.
3. Add white beets to the pressure cooker, with just enough water to cover them.
4. Add salt.
5. Secure the lid and maintain high pressure for 10-15 minutes.
6. Quick-release the pressure.
7. Add greens and cover with the hot water.
8. Close the lid and let them rest in the hot water for 5 minutes. Do not return to heat.
9. Put the greens and beets in a strainer.
10. Cut the beets into pieces.
11. In a sauté pan, heat olive oil.
12. Add beets and let them sit in the oil, do not mix.
13. Add garlic and the beet greens until tender.
14. Plate and serve with a squirt of fresh lemon juice.

Nutrition Info (Per Serving):
Calories - 105
Protein - 3
Fat - 11
Carbs - 15
Fiber - 3

Maple-Glazed Carrots
Serves: 8

Time: 3-4 minutes

Two pounds of sweet carrots with raisins can feed about 12 people, making this side dish a great option for a big dinner party or holiday. In the pressure cooker, this veggies cook up in less than 5 minutes.

Ingredients:
2 pounds carrots
¼ cup raisins
1 tablespoon maple syrup
1 tablespoon butter
Pepper to taste

Directions:
1. Wash, peel, and cut the carrots on the diagonal.
2. Put the raisins and carrots in about 1 cup of water in the pressure cooker.
3. Secure lid and maintain low pressure for 3-4 minutes.
4. Quick-release the pressure.
5. Strain the carrots.
6. In the pressure cooker, melt the butter and maple syrup without turning the heat on - it will still be warm.
7. Mix and add the carrots.
8. Divide and serve with freshly-cracked pepper to taste.

Nutrition Info (Per Serving):
Calories - 113
Protein - 1
Fat - 3
Carbs - 21
Fiber - 4

Prosciutto-Wrapped Asparagus
Serves: 2-4
Time: 2-3 minutes

This classy side dish can also be a classy appetizer. It only uses two ingredients - the salty, thinly-sliced prosciutto and tender asparagus spears - and is ready in mere minutes.

Ingredients:
1 pound asparagus spears

8-ounces Prosciutto

Directions:
1. Add 1-2 cups of water to the pressure cooker.
2. Wrap the asparagus in the meat.
3. To avoid using oil, lay down unwrapped spears in a single layer in the bottom of the steamer basket.
4. Place the wrapped spears on top.
5. Secure lid and cook on high pressure for 2-3 minutes.
6. Quick-release the pressure.
7. Take out the steamer basket right away so the veggies don't continue to cook.
8. Serve with a sprinkle of black pepper.

Nutrition Info (Per Serving):
Calories - 39
Protein - 3
Fat - 2
Carbs - 3
Fiber - 1

Mashed Acorn Squash
Serves: 4
Time: 20 minutes

Acorn squash is one of the tastiest vegetables out there. It's similar to butternut squash in terms of its sweet flesh, has very few calories and is high in fiber. This mashed recipe is a great alternative to mashed potatoes.

Ingredients:
2 acorn squash (halved, seeded, with the stems trimmed)
½ cup water
2 tablespoons butter
2 tablespoons brown sugar
1 teaspoon salt
½ teaspoon grated nutmeg
¼ teaspoon baking soda
Salt and pepper to taste

Directions:
1. Begin by sprinkling the fleshy side of the acorn squash with baking soda and salt.

2. Put the steamer basket in the pressure cooker and add ½ cup of water.
3. Put the squash inside.
4. Secure lid and cook on high pressure for 20 minutes.
5. Quick-release.
6. Let the squash cool.
7. When cooled, scrap out the flesh and add butter, brown sugar, and nutmeg.
8. Mash the squash until everything is blended and smooth.
9. Season further with salt and pepper if needed.

Nutrition Info (Per Serving):
Calories - 75
Protein - 1
Fat - 1
Carbs - 18
Fiber - 3

Acorn Squash Stuffed with Curried Chickpeas
Serves: 2
Time: 55 minutes

This hearty squash side dish could really stand on its own if you aren't very hungry, and it's Vegan-friendly. If you want to keep things lighter, you can leave out the brown rice and just use the curried chickpeas with the squash.

Ingredients:
2 cups water
1 small acorn squash, cut in half, with seeds removed
1 cup spinach
¾ cup dry chickpeas
½ cup chopped red onion
¼ cup brown rice (washed and soaked for 30 minutes)
4 chopped garlic cloves
2 chopped tomatoes
1 teaspoon olive oil
½ teaspoon cumin seeds
½ inch minced ginger
1 minced green chile
½ teaspoon turmeric
½ teaspoon garam masala
1 teaspoon lime juice

¼ teaspoon cayenne
Salt and pepper to taste

Directions:
1. Soak the chickpeas overnight.
2. Heat oil in a pressure cooker and add cumin seeds.
3. After about 1 minute, add the ginger, chile, onions, and garlic.
4. When translucent, add the spices and mix.
5. Add lime juice, greens, and tomato for 4-5 minutes.
6. Deglaze with a splash of water if any food bits are stuck to the sides.
7. Add 2 cups of water, rice, salt, cayenne, and chickpeas.
8. Put the cut squash in the steamer basket above the chickpea mixture.
9. Secure lid and cook on high pressure for 15-20 minutes.
10. Let the pressure decrease naturally.
11. Carefully remove squash and stuff with chickpea mixture.
12. Season to perfection!

Nutrition Info (Per Serving):
Calories - 75
Protein - 1
Fat - 1
Carbs - 18
Fiber - 3

Chapter 14 - Snack Foods

Pressure-Cooker "Gold Nugget" Potatoes
Serves: 2-3
Time: 15 minutes

When you're craving something salty, but don't want a snack as unhealthy as French fries, these cubed Yukon Gold potatoes will do just the trick. They're cooked in the pressure cooker first and then fried, so you get that real crispy goodness.

Ingredients:
1 pound Yukon Gold potatoes cut into 1-inch cubes
2 tablespoons butter
¼ cup minced Italian parsley
Kosher salt
Pepper
½ lemon

Directions:
1. Pour ½ cup water into your pressure cooker.
2. Add potatoes to the steamer basket.
3. Secure lid and cook on high pressure for 5 minutes.
4. Let the pressure decrease naturally.
5. Melt butter in a skillet over medium-high.
6. Once hot, add the potatoes.
7. Sprinkle on salt and pepper, and do not stir for 1 minute.
8. Flip the potatoes so they get brown on all sides.
9. Squeeze on lemon juice and add Italian parsley before serving.

Nutrition Info (Per Serving):
Calories - 268
Protein - 5
Fat - 23
Carbs - 39
Fiber - 4

Italian Popcorn
Serves: 6
Time: 10 minutes

Popcorn is a great snack, but it can be hard to find interesting flavors that aren't packed with artificial ingredients. This "Italian" popcorn uses a spice blend of basil, parsley, and garlic for a slightly gourmet taste.

Ingredients:
5 tablespoons unpopped popcorn
2 tablespoons olive oil
2 tablespoons vegetable oil
1 tablespoon basil
1 tablespoon parsley
½ teaspoon sea salt
¼ teaspoon garlic powder

Directions:
1. Measure out the spices, olive oil, and salt into a bowl.
2. Mix.
3. Pour the vegetable oil in the pressure cooker along with the popcorn.
4. Fasten lid and set to high heat.
5. With two hot pads, shake the pressure cooker when you hear the popping.
6. Keep shaking until you don't hear any more pops for about 5 seconds.
7. Remove from the heat.
8. With your head turned away and hot pads still on, open the lid.
9. Pour in the spice/oil mixture and stir.
10. Pour into bowls and serve!

Nutrition Info (Per Serving):
Calories - 84
Protein - 0
Fat - 10
Carbs - 16
Fiber - 3

Classic Artichoke Dip
Serves: 2
Time: 15-20 minutes

Artichoke dip is a game-day staple for a lot of people. It's warm, rich, and much healthier than sour cream or cheese-based dips. This recipe uses non-fat yogurt, too, which helps cut some calories. You get about 4 cups of dip, which is a good amount for two people, though you can feed more if there are other snacks available.

Ingredients:
1 cup water
1 pound baby artichokes
2 cloves smashed garlic cloves
½ cup quick-soaked cannellini beans
¾ cup plain non-fat yogurt
¾ cup grated Parmesan cheese
½ lemon
Salt and pepper to taste

Directions:
1. Pour 1 cup of water in the pressure cooker and add beans
2. Prepare the artichokes by taking off the outer leaves, leaving the inner part.
3. Trim the stubs and cut the top ⅓ of the artichoke off.
4. Rub a cut lemon on the outside and put in the pressure cooker.
5. Secure the lid and cook for 15-20 minutes on high pressure.
6. Let the pressure come down naturally before opening.
7. Add the garlic powder, yogurt, cheese, salt, and pepper.
8. Blend with a hand blender (or move everything to a regular blender).
9. You can eat right away, or refrigerate. You can also freeze it, and it will keep for 3 months!

Nutrition Info (Per Serving):
Calories - 180
Protein - 4
Fat - 20
Carbs - 8
Fiber - 3.6

Sweet 'n Tender BBQ Sausage Bites
Serves: 20
Time: 25 minutes

These smoky, sweet sausages are perfect for an appetizer or included as one of your party snacks. Thanks to the pressure cooker, you can make a big batch that serves 20 in under a half hour!

Ingredients:
2 pounds of smoked breakfast sausage
A sweet BBQ sauce
½ tablespoon brown sugar
½ tablespoon lemon juice

Directions:
1. Cut sausage into 1-inch pieces.
2. Place sausage bites in pressure cooker and add just enough water so the meat is covered.
3. Secure lid and maintain high pressure for 10 minutes.
4. Drain.
5. Mix the BBQ sauce with sugar and lemon.
6. Pour over the sausage.
7. Serve with toothpicks.

Nutrition Info (Per Serving):
Calories - 157
Protein - 6
Fat - 10
Carbs - 8
Fiber - 0

Boiled Peanuts
Serves: 10
Time: 45 minutes

Boiled peanuts are a Southern treat and healthier than their roasted or raw forms. This is because boiled peanuts are younger, and boiling them in the shells preserves antioxidants. They are a tender, salty snack great for any movie night!

Ingredients:
3 pounds raw peanuts in the shell (must have "green" or "raw" in the name)
1 6-ounce bottle of hot sauce
¾ cup salt

Directions:
1. Soak peanuts for 2-3 hours.
2. When ready, put everything in the pressure cooker with just enough water to cover them.

3. Secure the lid on your pressure cooker and cook at 10 psi for 45 minutes.
4. Let the pressure decrease naturally.
5. Drain and serve right away for tastiest results!

Nutrition Info (Per Serving/1 cup):
Calories - 200
Protein - 9
Fat - 14
Carbs - 13
Fiber - 6

Sweet Bourbon Chicken Wings
Serves: 3
Time: 25

These succulent chicken wings are smoky and sweet, with smoked paprika, honey, brown sugar, and cayenne. It also uses a bit of bourbon for a little extra kick. If everyone has 4-5 wings, this recipe should feed about three people.

Ingredients:
¾ cup water
2 pounds chicken wings
1 cup BBQ sauce
¼ cup bourbon
1 tablespoon honey
1 tablespoon brown sugar
1-2 teaspoons smoked paprika
1-2 teaspoons liquid smoke
¼ teaspoon cayenne
Salt and pepper

Directions:
1. Pat the wings dry before adding to pressure cooker.
2. In a bowl, mix water, sauce, bourbon, liquid smoke, cayenne, paprika, brown sugar, honey, and a dash of salt and pepper.
3. Pour over the wings before securing the pressure cooker lid.
4. Cook on high pressure for 10 minutes.
5. Quick-release.
6. Preheat the oven broiler.
7. Line a pan with foil and put a cooling rack on top.
8. Spray rack.

9. Put the wings on the rack.
10. Set your pressure cooker to "browning."
11. Broil wings for 5 minutes on each side in the broiler.
12. Stir the sauce in the pressure cooker.
13. Once thickened, cover wings and broil again for 5 minutes.
14. Flip wings over, put on more sauce, and broil again. You want a nice char.
15. Serve with napkins!

Nutrition Info (Per Serving/1 cup):
Calories - 238
Protein - 19
Fat - 15
Carbs - 8
Fiber - 0

Applesauce in a Pressure Cooker
Serves: 14
Time: 14 minutes

A lot of the snacks so far have been salty, so this one is sweet. Homemade applesauce usually takes hours on a stove in a pot, but that time is cut drastically when you use the pressure cooker. Stick to apples that are good for cooking, like Jonagold, Golden Delicious, Red Delicious, or Honey Crisp.

Ingredients:
10 large apples (peeled, cored, and sliced)
¼ cup sugar
¼ cup water
1 teaspoon ground cinnamon

Directions:
1. Put the apples, water, sugar, and cinnamon in the pressure cooker.
2. Stir.
3. Maintain high pressure for 4 minutes.
4. Quick-release the pressure.
5. Stir until your applesauce has the texture you want. You can also use a blender if necessary.

Nutrition Info (Per Serving):
Calories - 149

Protein - 1
Fat - 1
Carbs - 38
Fiber - 7

Meatballs with Marinara

Serves: 4
Time: 15 minutes

These classic meatballs with a homemade sauce are a fantastic appetizer or snack. You get 12 meatballs total, so four people get three meatballs each. For more, you can always double the recipe.

Ingredients:
1 pound meatloaf mix (ground beef and pork)
1 big egg
3 tablespoons minced parsley
½ cup grated Parmesan cheese
½ cup panko bread crumbs
¼ cup whole milk
1 onion
6 minced garlic cloves
2 (28-ounce) cans crushed tomatoes
2 tablespoons olive soil
2 teaspoons dried oregano
¼ teaspoon red pepper flakes
A little sugar
Salt and pepper to taste

Directions:
1. To make the sauce, begin by heating olive oil in the pressure cooker.
2. Add onion and salt and sauté for 5 minutes.
3. Next, mix in the oregano, red pepper flakes, and ⅔ of the garlic for 30 seconds.
4. Add crushed tomatoes and scrap away any stuck bits.
5. Reduce heat and simmer for 10 minutes or so.
6. Season with salt, pepper, and sugar to taste.
7. For the meatballs, mix the panko and milk in a bowl.
8. Mix in the meat, parsley, egg, garlic, cheese, and some salt and pepper with your hands.
9. Form into 12 meatballs and add to the pressure cooker and sauce.

10. Secure lid and cook on high pressure for 5 minutes.
11. Quick-release the pressure.
12. Garnish with basil and serve!

Nutrition Info (Per Serving):
Calories - 550
Protein - 38
Fat - 23
Carbs - 55
Fiber - 15

Homemade Hummus
Serves: 6-8
Time: 30 minutes

This chickpea-based, garlicky dip is a Middle Eastern staple. It is often served with warm pita bread and in sandwiches, like people use mayonnaise. It is a healthier option than other game-day dips, as well as more interesting. In terms of the ingredient list, you can find Tahini at any grocery store, or you can make your own.

Ingredients:
1 cup dry chickpeas (quick-soaked)
3-4 garlic cloves
2 big tablespoons Tahini
1 bay leaf
1 juiced lemon
½ bunch chopped parsley
½ teaspoon salt
¼ teaspoon cumin
Dash of paprika
Olive oil

Directions:
1. Give the chickpeas a quick rinse and add to pressure cooker.
2. Pour in 6 cups of water.
3. Add two of the crushed garlic cloves and the bay leaf.
4. Secure lid and cook at high pressure for 15-18 minutes (15 on a stove top, 18 for electric).
5. Let the pressure decrease naturally.
6. Drain the chickpeas, and keep the liquid.
7. Pick out the bay leaf.

8. Puree the chickpeas and add ½ cup of the cooking liquid with the Tahini, lemon juice, cumin, and 1-2 fresh garlic cloves.
9. If it isn't creamy enough, add a bit more of the cooking liquid.
10. Add some salt to taste.
11. To plate, create a dent in the center of the hummus and pour in some olive oil. Sprinkle with paprika and add parsley.

To make your own Tahini:
Toast 1 cup of hulled sesame seeds for 3-5 minutes in a wide saucepan with no oil. Remove from heat and let them cool. When cool, add to a food processor until they take on a crumb-like texture. Add 3 tablespoons of a light olive oil and process again. It should be smooth and pour easily, without grit. Add more oil if needed, and season to taste with salt. To store, keep covered in the fridge for up to 1 month. If you notice that it starts to separate, just stir before use.

Nutrition Info (Per Serving):
Calories - 109
Protein - 4
Fat -3.8
Carbs - .2
Fiber - 3.3

BBQ Brisket Sliders
Serves: 3-4
Time: 60 minutes

With just four ingredients, you can make tender, juicy BBQ brisket that is perfect for sliders. Serve with coleslaw, lettuce, tomato, and any other accompaniments that your heart desires. If you're going gluten-free, you can wrap the brisket in a big, crispy lettuce leaf or just eat it with a fork.

Ingredients:
3 pounds beef brisket
2 cups beef broth
1 cup BBQ sauce
½ cup BBQ sauce

Directions:

1. Pour the broth into the pressure cooker and add the brisket.
2. Cover with 1 cup of BBQ sauce.
3. Lock the pressure cooker and cook on high pressure for 60 minutes.
4. Carefully remove the meat and shred.
5. Add another ½ of BBQ sauce and about 1 cup of the cooking liquid.
6. Mix well.
7. Taste and add some seasonings (red pepper flakes, chile powder) if you want more heat.

Nutrition Info (Per Serving/Meat only):
Calories - 751
Protein - 91
Fat -23
Carbs - 40
Fiber - 0

Pressure-Cooker Pigs in a Blanket
Serves: 4
Time: 1 hour, 10 minutes

Pigs in a blanket are a classic childhood food. This version makes things a little more adult, though. Instead of a hot dog, you use a piece of tender steak wrapped in bacon, topped with a slice of onion. Coat in some flour, pop in the pressure cooker, and you've got a tasty, high-protein snack.

Ingredients:
1 pound boneless round steak
2 slices bacon
1 thinly-sliced onion
2 tablespoons corn oil
½ cup water
1 can condensed tomato soup
1 bay leaf
¼ cup all-purpose flour
Salt and pepper

Directions:
1. Cut steak into four long pieces and pound flat.
2. Season with salt and pepper.
3. Cut bacon strips in half and put on the beef.

4. Top with a slice of onion.
5. Roll up and stick in a toothpick.
6. Roll in flour.
7. In your pressure cooker, heat oil.
8. Brown rolls on all sides.
9. Pour in the tomato soup. For any soup left in the can, pour in water and pour into pressure cooker.
10. Toss in a bay leaf.
11. Secure lid and cook on high pressure for 30 minutes.
12. Let the pressure drop on its own.
13. When ready, serve with the toothpicks.

Nutrition Info (Per Serving):
Calories - 299
Protein - 21
Fat - 14.4
Carbs - 21.4
Fiber - 1.5

Chapter 15 - Desserts

Pressure-Cooker Peach Cobbler
Serves: 6-8
Time: About 10 minutes

You can make peach cobbler any time of year, but using fresh peaches during their peak season in July and August results in the best peach cobbler. Enjoy with some vanilla frozen yogurt or with a cup of coffee at breakfast.

Ingredients:
12 fresh peeled and pitted fresh peaches (cut in 1-inch pieces)
3 tablespoons cornstarch
¾ cup water
¼ cup sugar
¼ cup brown sugar
2 teaspoons lemon juice
¼ teaspoon cinnamon
2 ⅓ cups baking mix
½ cup milk
4 ½ tablespoons sugar, divided
3 tablespoons melted butter
1 teaspoon vanilla
½ teaspoon cinnamon

Directions;
1. In a bowl, mix the peaches, sugars, lemon juice, cornstarch, water, and cinnamon.
2. Pour into a pressure cooker.
3. For the topping, mix the baking mix, vanilla, milk, butter, and three tablespoons of sugar in a separate bowl.
4. In a third bowl, mix the cinnamon and rest of the sugar.
5. Spoon the baking mix topping unto the peaches and sprinkle with cinnamon sugar mixture.
6. Close up the pressure cooker lid tightly and maintain high pressure for 10 minutes.
7. Remove from heat and let the pressure decrease naturally.
8. Serve warm with ice cream, frozen yogurt, or on its own!

Nutrition Info (Per Serving):
Calories - 315

Protein - 4.8
Fat - .4
Carbs - 74.7
Fiber - 2

Fudgy Brownies
Serves: 1
Time: 10 minutes

I'm sure you are familiar with those brownie-in-a-mug recipes where you nuke a few ingredients in the microwave. Those have their place and usually turn out ok, but for a perfect, fudgy brownie in very little time, a pressure cooker is the way to go. It takes a little longer than microwave-mug brownies, but they turn out much better.

Ingredients:
3 tablespoons flour
3-4 drops of vanilla extract
2 tablespoons cocoa powder
2 tablespoons powdered sugar
1 tablespoon peanut butter
1 tablespoon oil
A splash of milk
Chopped walnuts (optional)

Directions:
1. Mix everything in a bowl and shake through a sieve.
2. Add the wet ingredients and mix together.
3. For a smoother consistency, add a splash of milk and whisk.
4. Preheat the pressure cooker for 5 minutes.
5. Grease a pressure-cooker safe baking bowl and pour in the brownie batter.
6. Place in the pressure cooker and cook for 10 minutes on high pressure.
7. Quick-release the pressure.
8. Carefully remove the bowl.
9. You can eat right from the bowl with a scoop of vanilla ice cream if you want!

Nutrition Info (Per Serving):
Calories - 410
Protein - 9

Fat - 23
Carbs - 43
Fiber - 0

Coconut Rice Pudding
Serves: 4
Time: 15-25 minutes

Rice pudding can be served warm or cold, and it's delicious either way. If you're feeling cozy, warm rice pudding is like sweet porridge, and when it's cold, it's a refreshing treat on a hot summer morning. This recipe adds a little twist with coconut milk and orange zest for an even more tropical taste.

Ingredients:
3 cups unsweetened coconut milk
2 cups unsweetened almond milk
1 cup water
1 cup Arborio rice (stick to this kind of rice, since it absorbs a lot more liquid)
2 cans sweetened condensed milk
3 cinnamon sticks
1 whole vanilla bean
3 strips orange zest
½ teaspoon freshly-ground cloves
Optional toppings: blueberries, honey, strawberries, nutmeg

Directions:
1. Pour of all the liquid ingredients minus the condensed milk into your pressure cooker.
2. If using an electric pressure cooker, hit start to start preheating the cooker.
3. Mix in the spices.
4. For the vanilla, slit down the middle and scrap out the beans. Add the whole pod, too.
5. Let the pressure cooker simmer all the aromatics together.
6. Turn off the heating element.
7. Add the rice and stir.
8. Secure the pressure cooker lid and program for 15 minutes on high pressure.
9. Once the timer goes off, remove from heat and let the pressure decrease naturally.
10. Pick out the zest, cinnamon sticks, and vanilla pod.

11. Add the two cans of sweetened condensed milk and stir well.
12. You can serve it warm right away if you want, or let it cool a little before storing in the fridge.

Nutrition Info (Per Serving):
Calories - 688
Protein - 16
Fat - 18
Carbs - 121
Fiber - 1.5

Pressure-Cooker Pumpkin Pie
Serves: 4
Time: 45-50 minutes

Pumpkin pie is a holiday favorite, especially on Thanksgiving, though many people like it during Christmas, too. This recipe is special because it uses crushed Pecan Sandies as the crust, making a crust so good you'll want to get it before the rest of the pie is done. The filling is also super delicious, and easy. It only uses six ingredients, and the actual cooking time is just over a half hour.

Ingredients:
½ cup crushed Pecan Sandies
2 tablespoons melted butter
⅓ cup chopped, toasted pecans
1 ½ cups solid pack pumpkin
½ cup light brown sugar
½ cup evaporated milk
1 beaten egg
1 ½ teaspoons pumpkin pie spice
½ teaspoon salt

Directions:
1. Coat a 7-inch springform pan with a non-stick spray.
2. Combine cookie crumbs, butter, and chopped pecans in a bowl.
3. Spread this mixture on the bottom of the pie pan and up an inch on the sides. Freeze for 10 minutes.
4. Meanwhile, mix salt, pumpkin pie spice, and sugar in another bowl. Whisk in the pumpkin puree, evaporated milk, and egg.
5. Pour this into the pie crust.

6. Cover the top of the pan with foil.
7. In your pressure cooker, add 1 cup of water and put a trivet in the bottom for the pan.
8. Close the pressure cooker lid and lock in place. Cook on high pressure for 35 minutes.
9. When ready, let the pressure go down naturally for 10 minutes.
10. Quick-release the rest of the pressure.
11. If the middle of the pie is set, it's ready. If not, cook for another 5 minutes.
12. Cool the pie and take off the foil.
13. When cool, cover with plastic wrap at least for 4 hours before eating.
14. Serve with whipped cream and enjoy!

Nutrition Info (Per Serving):
Calories - 316
Protein - 7
Fat - 4.9
Carbs - 40.9
Fiber - 3.9

Key Lime Pie
Serves: 8
Time: 25 minutes

Key lime pie is a perfect summer dessert. The chilly tartness combines with a sweet, buttery graham-cracker crust for a refreshing, delicious treat. To make this pie in a pressure cooker, just be sure you have a springform pan and a trivet for the pan to rest on while it's in the cooker.

Ingredients:
¾ cup graham-cracker crumbs
3 tablespoons melted butter, unsalted
1 tablespoon sugar
4 large eggs
1 can (14-ounces) sweetened condensed milk
½ cup fresh key lime juice
⅓ sour cream
2 tablespoons grated key lime zest

Directions:

1. Coat a 7-inch springform pan with non-stick spray.
2. In a bowl, mix the butter, sugar, and graham cracker crumbs.
3. Press into the pan, so it's even on the bottom and up an inch around the sides.
4. Put the crust in the freezer for 10 minutes.
5. In another bowl, beat the egg yolks.
6. Slowly beat in the sweetened condensed milk.
7. Slowly add lime juice and mix until smooth.
8. Add the sour cream and lime zest.
9. Pour this batter into the pan and cover with foil.
10. Add 1 cup of water to the pressure cooker and put the pie pan on a trivet inside the cooker.
11. Secure the lid.
12. Cook for 15 minutes on high pressure.
13. Let the pressure decrease naturally for 10 minutes, and then quick-release the rest.
14. Move the pie pan to a wire rack so it can cool. Take off the foil.
15. If the middle of the pie isn't set, cook for another 5 minutes.
16. Cool covered in the fridge for 4 hours.
17. Serve with a dollop of fresh whipped cream.

Nutrition Info (Per Serving):
Calories - 553
Protein - 11
Fat - 21
Carbs - 85
Fiber - 1

Pressure-Cooked Baked Apples
Serves: 6
Time: 20 minutes

Apples are naturally sweet, and they only become sweeter when they're baked in a pressure cooker. All you need for this recipe to be delicious is apples and some extra ingredients like raisins and red wine; the cooking liquid becomes the sauce.

Ingredients:
6 cored apples
1 cup red wine
½ cup raw demerara sugar
¼ cup raisins

1 teaspoon cinnamon powder

Directions:
1. Put the apples in the pressure cooker.
2. Add wine, sugar, raisins, and cinnamon.
3. Secure the pressure cooker lid.
4. Cook for 10 minutes on high pressure.
5. Let the pressure come down naturally.
6. When ready, put apples in serving bowls and pour cooking liquid over them.

Nutrition Info (Per Serving):
Calories - 188.7
Protein - .6
Fat - .3
Carbs - 41.9
Fiber - 3.8

Egg-Free Chocolate Cake
Serves: 4
Time: 45 minutes

For the dairy-intolerant, desserts can be tricky. However, this moist chocolate cake doesn't use eggs, so you don't have to worry. With just a handful of ingredients, you can make the best homemade chocolate cake you've ever eaten.

Ingredients:
1 cup all-purpose flour
¾ cup hot water
⅓ cup sugar
¼ cup vegetable oil
3 tablespoons cocoa powder
1 tablespoon lemon juice
½ teaspoon baking powder
¼ teaspoon baking soda
¼ teaspoon vanilla extract

Directions:
1. Mix the sugar, water, oil, and vanilla in a bowl.
2. Stir in all the wet ingredients and mix until the sugar dissolves.

3. Sift the flour, cocoa powder, baking soda, and baking powder into the wet ingredients.
4. Mix well.
5. Preheat the pressure cooker.
6. While this is heating up, prepare a cake tin with cooking oil.
7. Add lime juice to the cake batter and pour into the baking tin.
8. Put an empty pot into the pressure cooker and then put the cake tin on top. The cake tin should not touch the bottom of the pressure cooker.
9. Secure the lid.
10. Bake on medium heat for 5 minutes.
11. Lower the heat and cook for another 30.
12. When that time is up, turn off the cooker and let the cake sit in there for another 5 minutes.
13. Check the cake with a toothpick. If it comes out clean in the middle, it's done.
14. Let the cake cool for 10 minutes.
15. Remove the cake from the tin by running a knife along the edges and flipping over unto a plate.
16. Let it cool before icing or serving.

Nutrition Info (Per Serving):
Calories - 304
Protein - 4
Fat -15
Carbs - 42
Fiber - 0

5-Minute Nut Fudge
Serves: 8
Time: 5 minutes

These chocolate fudge drops are super easy to make and perfect for when you need a dessert fast. Chopped walnuts add some crunch to the smooth chocolate. If you don't like walnuts, you can sub in other chopped nuts, like almonds.

Ingredients:
2 cups water
1 cup chopped walnuts
12-ounces of semi-sweet chocolate chips
14-ounces of sweetened condensed milk

1 teaspoon vanilla

Directions:
1. Mix the chocolate chips with the condensed milk in a stainless steel bowl. It should fit into the pressure cooker.
2. Cover with foil.
3. Pour water into the pressure cooker.
4. Place the bowl of chocolate on top of the cooking rack in the pressure cooker.
5. Secure lid.
6. Cook on high pressure for 5 minutes.
7. Use the cold water release to bring down the pressure.
8. Take out the bowl.
9. Fold in the vanilla and chopped nuts, mixing until smooth.
10. Using a teaspoon, measure out the chocolate drops in paper candy cups. You can also use mini muffin wrappers.
11. Cool until hard before eating.

Nutrition Info (Per Serving):
Calories - 450
Protein - 9
Fat -25
Carbs - 57
Fiber - 0

Baked Chocolate Custard
Serves: 6-8
Time: 30 minutes

This incredibly-rich baked chocolate custard is a great dessert for a classy dinner party. Instead of having to mess with preparing individual cups, you can make the whole thing in one round dish, and there's enough for 6-8 people. For serving, consider fresh-cut strawberries.

Ingredients:
6 egg yolks
Almost 3 cups of dark cooking chocolate, chopped
1.3 cups of cream (300 ml)
1 cup of full cream milk (250 ml)
1 teaspoon vanilla extract

Directions:

1. Simmer the milk, cream, sugar, and vanilla.
2. Stir.
3. Remove from heat and add the chopped chocolate.
4. When it's melted, it should look like a chocolate sauce.
5. Whisk egg yolks separately before slowly adding to the chocolate.
6. Pour 4 cups of water into the pressure cooker.
7. Pour the chocolate into a round pressure cooker-safe dish and put in the pressure cooker on top of a trivet.
8. Cook on high pressure for 30 minutes.
9. Serve and enjoy!

Nutrition Info (Per Serving):
Calories - 553
Protein - 8
Fat -32
Carbs - 52
Fiber - 0

Amaretti-Stuffed Peaches
Serves: 6
Time: 3-5 minutes

Sweet, juicy peaches stuffed with Amaretti cookies and almonds, cooked in butter and wine. My mouth is watering, just thinking about this dessert. It's a great option for summer, when you don't want to spend a lot of time mixing and measuring, and peaches are in-season. These are also a pretty healthy dessert option and add up to less than 200 calories per stuffed peach half.

Ingredients:
3 peaches
1 cup crumbled Amaretti cookies
1 cup red wine
4 tablespoons sugar
2 tablespoons almonds
2 tablespoons melted butter
1 teaspoon lemon zest

Directions:
1. Pour wine and sugar into the pressure cooker.
2. In a chopper, crumble the cookies and almonds.
3. Mix in lemon zest and melted butter.

4. Prepare and wash peaches.
5. Slice in half and take out the pit. Make that hole a bit bigger with a melon-baller.
6. Fill with the cookie mixture.
7. Put the peaches in the steamer basket in the pressure cooker.
8. Secure and lock lid and cook at high pressure for 3 minutes.
9. Quick-release the pressure.
10. Carefully remove the peaches.
11. Keep cooking the liquid uncovered until it becomes syrupy and thick.
12. Pour over peaches.
13. Serve with whipped cream or ice cream!

Nutrition Info (Per Serving):
Calories - 157
Protein - 2
Fat -5
Carbs - 21
Fiber - 1.5

Chestnut-Hazelnut Truffles
Serves: 15
Time: 25 minutes

Delicate and rich truffles make the perfect dessert or hostess gift, especially when they're homemade. This recipe calls for two kinds of nuts - chestnuts and hazelnuts - and turns up the heat with rum liquor. You get about 30-48 truffles, depending on how big you make them.

Ingredients:
2 pounds fresh chestnuts
1 cup whole hazelnuts, unshelled
½ cup sugar
10 tablespoons butter
½ cup rum liquor
¼ cup sweet chocolate powder (or bitter)

Directions:
1. Wash chestnuts, but do not peel. Put in the pressure cooker.
2. Cover with 2 inches of water and two tablespoons sugar.
3. Secure the lid.
4. Cook on high pressure for 8 minutes.

5.   Let the pressure decrease naturally when the timer goes off.
6.   You want the chestnuts to still be warm and moist when you take them out.
7.   Slice in half and get out the nut flesh with the handle of your teaspoon measurement.
8.   In this pulpy mixture, add rum, melted butter, and sugar.
9.   Mash well.
10. Form truffle balls with your hands and push a whole hazelnut inside.
11. Roll again, this time in cocoa powder, so the ball becomes tighter.
12. Chill well before serving.

Nutrition Info (Per Serving):
Calories - 314
Protein - 4
Fat -14
Carbs - 41
Fiber - 1

Pressure-Cooker Mocha Cheesecake
Serves: 8
Time: 30 minutes

Cheesecake is an awesome dessert. It's fluffy, sweet, and when you combine it with espresso and Kahlua, it becomes sophisticated and unique. This recipe makes a chocolate graham-cracker crust, too, which is my favorite part of the whole dessert.

Ingredients:
4 cups softened cream cheese
2 cups semi-sweet chocolate chips
¾ chocolate graham cracker crumbs
2 eggs
1 cup sugar
4 tablespoons whipping cream
3 tablespoons melted butter
3 tablespoons espresso
3 tablespoons Kahlua
1 teaspoon vanilla

Directions:

1. Grease a 6-cup soufflé dish (or a springform pan). Line with greased foil.
2. Mix butter, crumbs, and ¼ of the sugar.
3. Press mixture into the pan and then chill.
4. Beat the rest of the sugar with the cream cheese until it's smooth.
5. As you're beating, add one egg at a time.
6. Lastly, beat in the whipping cream and vanilla.
7. In a saucepan, melt the chocolate chips, espresso, and Kahlua.
8. Pour this chocolate mixture over the cream cheese mixture and combine.
9. Pour into the chilled crust pan.
10. Pour 1 ½ cups of water in your pressure cooker.
11. Set down a trivet, and place the cheesecake pan on top.
12. Secure the lid and maintain high pressure for 15 minutes.
13. Let the pressure decrease naturally.
14. Once all the pressure is gone, take off the lid.
15. Cool the cheesecake on a rack.
16. Cover and let the cake chill overnight or at least 4 hours before serving.

Nutrition Info (Per Serving):
Calories - 564
Protein - 9
Fat -44
Carbs - 38
Fiber – 5

Epilogue

I hope that you see how amazing a pressure cooker can be! If you've never used one, it can seem like a strange and complicated piece of kitchen equipment, so let the first few chapters of this book make things less scary. We went over the history of the pressure cooker, which involved a lot of explosions and tweaking to make the tool safe. Though it stopped being popular for a few years, the pressure cooker made a comeback, and can be found in many kitchens both professional and amateur. Pressure cookers work by raising the boiling point of water by using pressure. When you secure that lid real tightly on your pressure cooker, you're harnessing the power of pressure.

Pressure cooking is fast, convenient, and healthier than other cooking methods! This is because the fast cooking time keeps all the nutrients from seeping out of the food, and creates food that are more easily absorbed by your system. But what pressure cooker should you get? Stove top pressure cookers are more powerful and cook food faster, but you have to watch them in order to maintain the right amount of pressure. Electric pressure cookers monitor themselves, and while they don't generate really high levels of pressure like stove top cookers, they do have convenient settings like "sauté," "simmer," and so on.

Using a pressure cooker can seem intimidating, so it's important to know how to use one and what certain words mean. Chapter 4 went over terms like "quick-release," which is when you manually release the pressure. Following a recipe's instructions on how to release the pressure is critical and affects how the recipe will turn out. Whether the recipe calls for the "cold water release" or "normal release," you should know which is which.

Chapter 5 gave you a guide on how to convert slow cooker recipes to your pressure cooker. Some critical points to remember include only putting in as much liquid as you want to end up with in the final result, and figuring out the time difference between a slow cooker and pressure cooker. I have included a time conversion chart index at the end of the book, so you get a good idea of how long to cook pressure-cooker favorites like beef ribs, beans, and rice.

The last chapter before the recipe portion of the book covered safety and pantry tips. A pressure cooker can be dangerous because of how hot it gets, so it's important to always use hot pads. Also, always turn your body away from the pressure cooker when you're opening it or quick-releasing the pressure. That steam is extremely hot and will scald you. In terms of what to shop for when you have a pressure cooker, tough cuts of meat are transformed, and tough-to-digest foods like beans are easier and healthier when prepared in a pressure cooker.

I love pressure cookers and I love all the recipes I've included in this book. I have done my best to give you a huge variety of choices, from breakfasts, to chicken, beef, seafood, and vegan entrees, as well as sides, snack foods, and desserts. You can make Italian, Indian, and Asian dishes easily and quickly in a pressure cooker, and expand your food horizons further than you thought possible before owning a pressure cooker. I wish you the best of luck in your cooking adventures, and am positive that whoever you cook for will be extremely impressed!

Index 1- Time Conversion Charts

Food	Electric Pressure Cooker (10-12 psi) Time	Stove top Pressure Cooker (13-15 psi) Time	Pressure Selection
Beef (brisket)	70	50	High
Beef (ground)	6	6	High
Beef (ribs)	60	45	High
Chicken breast (boneless)	1	1	High
Chicken (ground)	5	4	High
Chicken (whole)	20	15	High
Eggs (poached)	2	2	Low
Lamb chops	7	3	High
Pork chops	8	6	High
Pork ribs	20	15	High
Pork sausage	10	8	High
Roast beef (medium)	8 to 10	8	High
Turkey breast (sliced)	7 to 9	7	High
Turkey leg	35	30	High
Fish fillet	3	2	Low
Salmon	6	5	Low
Shrimp	2	1	Low
Trout	12	8	Low
Oats (steel-cut)	3	3	High
Quinoa	1	1	High
Brown rice	20	18	High
Jasmine rice (rinsed)	1	1	Low or high
White (long-grain) rice	3	3	Low or high
Artichoke hearts	3	3	Low or high
Broccoli	3 to 5	3 to 5	Low or high

Carrots (sliced)	1 to 2	1 to 2	Low or high
Cauliflower (florets)	2 to 3	2 to 3	Low or high
Corn on the cob	5	5	Low or high
Onions	3	3	Low or high
Peas (fresh or frozen)	2 to 3	2 to 3	Low or high
Bell peppers	3 to 4	3 to 4	Low or high
Whole sweet potatoes	15	10	High
Butternut squash (halves)	6	6	Low or high
Apples	3	2	High
Black beans (soaked)	6	4	High
White beans (soaked)	8	6	High

Index 2- Canning Foods

Canning food is typically done with a pressure canner, so what's the difference between a canner and a pressure cooker? The only real difference is the size - pressure canners are bigger, so you can fit jars of food inside of it. You can use a pressure canner for preparing regular food, too, but most people find them too big for that task.

There are some pressure cookers that double as pressure canners, so it's useful to know how to can food. You will need the following equipment:
- A pressure canner
- Glass jars, lids, and bands
- A jar lifter
- A recipe
- Fresh ingredients
- Normal kitchen equipment (wooden spoons, ladles, etc.)

Step 1: Read the recipe and gather the necessary equipment and ingredients.

Step 2: Make sure the jars are in working order and there are no cracks or sharp edges. Make sure the sealing on everything is tight, and the bands fit.

Step 3: Wash and rinse the jars well.

Step 4: Keep the jars in hot (not boiling) water. Do this by keeping them in a large saucepan that's filled halfway with water. Simmer over medium heat. Leave the lids and bands on the counter, as you will need to handle these.

Step 5: Fill your pressure canner with 2-3 inches of water. Simmer.

Step 6: Get your food ready according to the recipe you're following.

Step 7: Using a Jar Lifter, take out the jar and fill with food using a funnel. If you need to remove air bubbles, follow the instructions using a Bubble Remover tool.

Step 8: Clean the rims and threads of jars.

Step 9: Put the lids on the jars so the sealing part touches the jar rim. Adjust band so it fits very tightly.

Step 10: Place jars in canner.

Step 11: Lock the pressure canner lid.

Step 12: Open the vent pipe and adjust heat to medium-high. Let the steam vent out for 10 minutes before closing the vent.

Step 13: Adjust heat until the proper pressure is reached.

Step 14: Follow the instructions for time and pressure.

Step 15: Once time is up, remove pressure canner from heat. Let the pressure decrease naturally.

Step 16: Open the canner, but be sure to turn away from canner. Wait 10 minutes until jars cool.

Step 17: Remove from canner and place on a towel upright so the jars don't break. Don't touch for 12-24 hours.

Step 18: Once time is up, check the seals. The lids should not flex when you poke the center, and you should not be able to lift the lid off. If the lid hasn't sealed, refrigerate right away.

Step 19: Wipe the jars and lids clean and store in a dark, dry, cool place for 1 year.

I hope the book was able to teach you how pressure cooking can simplify your everyday life.

If you enjoyed this book, then I'd like to ask you for a favor, would you be kind enough to leave a review for this book on Amazon? It'd be greatly appreciated!

Also, I would love to give you a bonus. Please email me at vanessa.olsen400p@gmail.com to avail the FREE Paleo Diet book.

Please check out my other books in Amazon:
- **Ketogenic Diet** - Achieve Rapid Weight Loss while Gaining Incredible Health and Energy
- **Ketogenic Diet Cookbook** - 80 Easy, Delicious, and Healthy Recipes to Help You Lose Weight, Boost Your Energy, and Prevent Cancer, Stroke and Alzheimer's
- **Ketogenic Diet-2 in 1 Box Set** - A Complete Guide to the Ketogenic Diet-115 Amazing Recipes for Weight Loss and Improved Health
- **Mediterranean Diet for Beginners** - 50 Amazing Recipes for Weight Loss and Improved Health

- **Mediterranean Diet Cookbook** - 105 Easy, Irresistible, and Healthy Recipes for Weight Loss and Improved Quality of Life While Minimizing the Risk of Disease
- **Mediterranean Diet-2 in 1 Box Set** - A Comprehensive Guide to the Mediterranean Diet-155 Mouth-Watering and Healthy Recipes to Help You Lose Weight, Increase Your Energy Level and Prevent Disease

Thank you and good luck!

Made in the USA
Middletown, DE
22 February 2016